A Birder's Guide
to the
Coast of Maine

8/88
Rangeley Lake, ME.
Red-Breasted Mergansers
1 im. Loon
Ducks

6/94
Wells - accom Fishermans 'Catch
in marsh
Snowy Egret
Goose Rock Beach - many Piping Plovers
w/ young

A Birder's Guide
to the
Coast of Maine

Elizabeth Cary Pierson and Jan Erik Pierson

with a foreword by Olin Sewall Pettingill, Jr.

Maps by Anne Kilham

Down East Books   Camden, Maine

ISBN 0-89272-118-9
Library of Congress Catalog Card Number 81-67953

Design: Anne Kilham
Composition: J.S. McCarthy Co.
Printed in the United States of America

Down East Books   Camden, Maine

10   9   8   7   6   5   4   3

Cover photograph: Atlantic Puffin, *Fratercula arctica*

CONTENTS

Acknowledgments

No one writes a bird finding guide without the help of many friends. To Hank Tyler, who provided the inspiration and initial encouragement to write this book, we owe a special thanks. Peter Cannell, Norm Famous, and Chuck Huntington were especially generous with their editorial help. Others who willingly shared their time and knowledge were John Baxter, Sally K. Butcher, Bart Cadbury, the Canadian Wildlife Service, June Ficker, Margaret H. Hundley, Mark L. Libby, Mike Lucey, Mark McCollough, Maurice Mills, Doug Mullen and the March 1981 occupants of the Woodcock Shack at Moosehorn, Lee Perry, Jeanne Gibson Rollins, Nellie Ross, Will Russell, Frank Sanford, Dorothy and Warren Spaulding, and Bill Townsend. To all these and many other friends we have birded with, our grateful thanks.

References we consulted often were *American Birds, An Annotated Checklist of Maine Birds* by Peter D. Vickery, *Maine Bird Life* edited by Mike Lucey, and *Maine Birds* by Ralph Palmer. The Maine Breeding Bird Atlas, directed by Peter Cannell, was another source of much information.

One source of help stands out far above any other. We especially thank Paul K. Donahue who gave tirelessly of his time, expertise, and encouragement. To Paul, more than to anyone else, we owe a very special debt.

Foreword

In no one area of the contiguous United States is the birder in more need of a guide than the coast of Maine, complicated by its scores of islands and by its countless indentations from wide bays and snug harbors to deceptively narrow inlets. There are birds galore, many obvious wherever sea and land meet, but certain species —those that the diligent birder is intent on finding — are generally restricted to particular islands or remote headlands, to outer harbors and waters far offshore, that require exacting directions to observe. Here is just such a *vade mecum.*

Relying on their personal familiarity with the geography and birds of the Maine coast from Kittery Point "down east" to Quoddy Head and Eastport, Elizabeth and Jan Pierson have carefully selected those sites that will yield in one season or another all the species one can expect to see. And, most important, they have spared no detail in their directions as to when and how to reach the sites and have been generous in advice and precaution before any trip is undertaken.

Happy birding with the Piersons.

OLIN SEWALL PETTINGILL, JR.

Introduction

The coast is the most prominent feature of Maine, both physically and aesthetically. To birders it offers the greatest diversity, as very few species occuring in the state are not seen regularly along the coast. Thus it is here that this book focuses. The coast may not be the wildest or most remote part of the state, but certainly it is here that you can find the most diverse birding.

As of 1981 at least 395 species of birds are known to have occurred in Maine, 194 of which breed here and 69 of which are of vary rare or hypothetical occurrence. While Maine does not offer the diversity of habitat or birdlife found in some parts of the country, its variety of boreal and coastal species — few of which occur regularly elsewhere in the eastern United States — have long been of special interest to birders. Maine also is of interest as a transition zone in which many species approach their southern or northern limits.

The greatest diversity of birdlife in Maine is found during the breeding season and migration, while mid-winter is the best time to find many northern landbirds and waterbirds.

The Face of Maine

Comprising about 33,000 square miles, Maine is the largest of the six New England states, almost as large as the other five combined. Eighty-nine percent of it is forested, but the landscape is far from monotonous. The coast — which measures 230 miles from Kittery to Eastport as the crow flies but 3,500 miles if measured to include inlets, bays, and peninsulas — looks seaward to the Gulf of Maine, which extends from Cape Cod north to Cape Sable Island and east to Georges Bank. Scattered offshore are more than 2,000 islands, as dense a sprinkling as anywhere in the world. In addition to a rugged, surfbound coast, Maine also is distinguished by mountains that constitute a northeast extension of the Appalachians and rise from a few hundred feet to 5,269-foot Mt. Katahdin; more than 2,500 lakes and ponds; and some 5,000 rivers, of which the most prominent, from west to east, are the Saco, Androscoggin, Kennebec, Penobscot, St. Croix, and St. John.

Maine is the most sparsely populated state east of the Mississippi, with a population of just over 1 million. About half the population lives on the coast, mostly in the southwest, while much of northern and western Maine is uninhabited. Portland, with a population of about 62,000, is the largest city, followed by Lewiston and then Bangor. Forest products, fishing, tourism, and manufacturing are the backbone of the economy.

Geological History

Maine owes many of its topographical features to the effects of glaciation, and nowhere is this more apparent than on the coast. During the Ice Age or Pleistocene Epoch, which began about 1 million years ago, Maine was covered by glaciers 1 mile or more thick. This immense weight depressed both land and sea, perhaps as much as several hundred feet in some areas. Then, as the ice began to melt about 14,000 years ago, sea level rose and flooded the still-depressed land. The land is rising back up, but slowly, and the glaciers left in their wake what is known as a *drowned coast*. River valleys once miles from the sea now are fertile fishing grounds and the tops of former mountains now submerged form the multitude of Maine islands.

The landscape of Maine today reflects the geologic youthfulness of a coast scoured and sculpted by ice. From Kittery to the mouth of the Kennebec in Bath the coast is low-lying with sand beaches and salt marshes typical of the coast further south. East of the Kennebec the coast is characterized by bold, rocky headlands and promontories that the sea has not yet had time to erode. The sediments needed to seal off drowned valleys are yielded slowly, and the marshes and beaches seen further south become smaller and more infrequent as you move east up the coast. As the landscape changes from Kittery to Calais, so does the birdlife.

In the flora of Maine are written more reminders of the Ice Age. When the glaciers retreated they left behind a rubble of rock and mud. The first plants to colonize this debris were mosses, lichens, and sedges — plants with few requirements other than a substrate on which to grow. Through the centuries they have stabilized the glacial till and slowly made soil out of rock. Rarely is the bedrock in Maine covered by more than a thin veneer of soil, though, and in many places it still remains exposed. For the most part, the vegetation along the coast must be hardy, fast-growing, and capable of surviving in highly acidic soil and a foggy, damp climate.

Coastal Habitats and Associated Breeding Birds

Islands
Numbering more than 2,000, these rocky islands range in size from 13,000-acre Mount Desert to innumerable ledges of less than an acre or two. Many of the outer islands are small and treeless, typically covered with grasses, herbs, ragweeds, goldenrods, and often impenetrable thickets of Bayberry and Red Raspberry. Like the mainland coast, most of the inner islands are covered with dense stands of Red and White Spruce, Balsam Fir, and scattered birches.

Characteristic breeders on Maine islands are Leach's Storm Petrel, Double-crested Cormorant, Common Eider, Greater Black-backed Gull, Herring Gull, Common and Arctic Terns, Razorbill, Black Guillemot, and Atlantic Puffin. On treeless islands you may also find Spotted Sandpipers and Savannah Sparrows nesting and if there is a lighthouse or some other building, Tree, Barn, or Cliff Swallows. On wooded islands Great Blue Herons, Osprey, and Northern Ravens may nest, in addition to many of the passerines you would expect to see on the mainland.

Sand Beaches

Maine has only 75 miles of sand beach, almost all of which is found west of the Kennebec River. American Beach Grass vegetates the foredunes, and behind it grow such typical beach plants as Dusty Miller, Beach Pea, Seaside Goldenrod, Bayberry, Rugosa Rose, and beyond the backdune, Pitch Pine.

    Small numbers of Little Terns and Piping Plovers nest along some beaches, and Spotted Sandpipers may nest along nearby tidal inlets. Savannah Sparrows often nest in the dune grass and Yellow Warblers, Common Yellowthroats, and Song Sparrows in nearby thickets. Pine Warblers may nest in the Pitch Pine.

Salt Marshes

Salt marsh acreage is small compared with that of other states along the Atlantic coast, and like the sand beaches, most of it is found west of the Kennebec. Scarborough Marsh, with about 3,000 acres, is the largest in the state. Like all salt marshes, those in Maine are a meeting place for land and sea. The predominant plant in the lower marsh is Salt Marsh Cord Grass. In the upper marsh, which is flooded only on a very high tide, grows the finer and much shorter Salt-meadow Grass, along with glassworts, Sea Lavender, Seaside Goldenrod, and Orach. In salt pans, the small depressions that trap and hold water on a high tide, grow glassworts, Orach, and Seaside Plantain. Black Grass and Spike Grass are found along the highest edges of the marsh.

    Though many birds feed in salt marshes, only a few actually nest in them. Sharp-tailed Sparrows typically nest in the Salt-meadow Grass, and at Scarborough Marsh Willets nest there too. On the upper marsh, where it is drier, you may find Northern Harriers and Savannah Sparrows nesting and in thickets that border the marsh Green Herons, Common Yellowthroats, and Song Sparrows.

White Pine and/or Deciduous Woods

On the sandy soils of the southern coast mixed stands of White Pine and deciduous trees are the predominant forest cover. Each year, as more and more farms are abandoned, this habitat grows more widespread. Mixed with the White Pine, or sometimes bordering it, are maples, birches, oaks, aspens, and beech. Mountain Ash, Mountain and Striped Maple, viburnums, and Witch Hazel are typical of the understory, while on the ground are found such species as Clintonia, Common Wood Sorrel, Star Flower, Goldthread, Twinflower, and Bunchberry.

Characteristic breeders in this habitat are

Northern Goshawk	Eastern Pewee
Sharp-shinned Hawk	Blue Jay
Cooper's Hawk	American Crow
Red-tailed Hawk	Black-capped Chickadee
Red-shouldered Hawk	White-breasted Nuthatch
Broad-winged Hawk	Brown Thrasher
Ruffed Grouse	Wood Thrush
Great Horned Owl	Hermit Thrush
Barred Owl	Veery
Saw-whet Owl	Red-eyed Vireo
Whip-poor-will	Black-and-white Warbler
Pileated Woodpecker	Chestnut-sided Warbler
Yellow-bellied Sapsucker	Pine Warbler
Hairy Woodpecker	American Redstart
Downy Woodpecker	Ovenbird
Great Crested Flycatcher	Scarlet Tanager
Least Flycatcher	Rose-breasted Grosbeak

Spruce-fir Woods

East of Penobscot Bay spruce-fir woods, often running right to the water's edge, dominate the coast. Dense stands of Red and White Spruce, Balsam Fir, and Eastern Hemlock, typically mixed with Tamarack, maples, birches, willows, poplars, and sometimes Atlantic White Cedar, create a world of stillness, dampness, and shade. The needle-strewn forest floor contributes to a highly acidic, nutrient-poor soil which supports a variety of ferns, mosses, mushrooms, and lichens.

Permanent residents of the spruce-fir forest are:

Spruce Grouse	Evening Grosbeak
Black-backed Three-toed	Purple Finch
Woodpecker	Pine Grosbeak
Northern Raven	Pine Siskin
Gray Jay	American Goldfinch
Black-capped Chickadee	Red Crossbill
Boreal Chickadee	White-winged Crossbill
Red-breasted Nuthatch	

Other characteristic species that nest in spruce-fir woods are:

Yellow-bellied Flycatcher	Magnolia Warbler
Olive-sided Flycatcher	Cape May Warbler
Brown Creeper	Yellow-rumped Warbler
Winter Wren	Black-throated Green Warbler
Swainson's Thrush	Blackburnian Warbler
Golden-crowned Kinglet	Bay-breasted Warbler
Ruby-crowned Kinglet	Blackpoll Warbler
Solitary Vireo	Northern Junco
Northern Parula Warbler	White-throated Sparrow

Bogs

Bogs become increasingly common east of Mount Desert Island. They are typical of areas where the underlying bedrock is granite, which yields few nutrients for plants. Characterized by a layer of Sphagnum Moss, high acidity, and stagnant or slow-moving water, they are specialized, self-contained environments. Sheep Laurel, Labrador Tea, Leatherleaf, Pitcher Plant, sundews, and lovely bog orchids are common ground plants, while Black Spruce, Tamarack, Balsam Fir, and Atlantic White Cedar are common trees. Yellow-bellied Flycatcher, Palm Warbler, and Lincoln's Sparrow are characteristic bog nesters. Boreal Chickadees, Ruby-crowned Kinglets, and a variety of other spruce-woods birds may nest around the edges of bogs.

Freshwater Marshes

Freshwater marshes are found all along the coast and are characterized by their extensive growths of cattails and Bulrushes. Unlike many similar marshes found further south along the coast, most of those in Maine are fairly small. Breeding birds associated with them include Pied-billed Grebe, Least Bittern (rare), American Bittern, Virginia Rail, Sora, Common Gallinule, American Coot, Common Snipe, Marsh Wren, Sedge Wren (rare), Red-winged Blackbird, and Swamp Sparrow.

The wet ground around marshes is often covered with a dense growth of one or more species of alders. Characteristic species which breed in these thickets are Alder Flycatcher, Tennessee Warbler, Yellow Warbler, Northern Waterthrush, Common Yellowthroat, Wilson's Warbler, and American Redstart.

Open Land

Wherever you go in Maine you will find fields, meadows, farmlands, orchards, and backyards, collectively referred to here as open land. Breeding birds in and around these areas are:

American Kestrel	Yellow Warbler
Mourning Dove	House Sparrow
Common Nighthawk	Bobolink
Eastern Kingbird	Eastern Meadowlark
Eastern Phoebe	Northern Oriole
Tree Swallow	Common Grackle
Barn Swallow	Brown-headed Cowbird
Cliff Swallow	Northern Cardinal (southern Maine)
Purple Martin	Indigo Bunting
House Wren	House Finch
Northern Mockingbird	Savannah Sparrow
Gray Catbird	Vesper Sparrow
American Robin	Chipping Sparrow
Eastern Bluebird	Field Sparrow
Cedar Waxwing	Song Sparrow
European Starling	

Migration

Most Maine birds are migratory since the climate is severe. Of 194 species known to nest in Maine, only about 55 typically winter-over. Even among these, many individuals within a species may undertake a true migration, while those that don't may undertake a limited migration, moving from northern to southern Maine, for example. While Maine may be the summering ground for many species that migrate south for the winter, it likewise is the southern wintering ground for some species that nest farther north, such as the Great Cormorant. Spring migration, when birds are en route to their nesting grounds, usually is more urgent and concentrated than fall migration, which by comparison is quite protracted. Augmented by first-year birds, fall migration can be especially impressive.

The coast is an important flyway for many migrants. The most interesting groups are: waterfowl, hawks, shorebirds, and landbirds.

Waterfowl

Waterfowl usually are the earliest migrants in spring and the latest in fall. Spring migration extends from about mid-March through at least April and fall migration from mid-September through November. Regular species along the coast, many of which winter-over, are Canada Goose, Brant, Snow Goose, Mallard, American Black Duck, Common Pintail, Green-winged and Blue-winged Teal, Wood Duck, Ring-necked Duck, Greater Scaup, Common Goldeneye, Bufflehead, Oldsquaw, Common Eider, White-winged, Surf, and Black Scoters, and Hooded, Common, and Red-breasted Mergansers. Often migrating in association with waterfowl are Common and Red-throated Loons, Red-necked and Horned Grebes, and Double-crested and Great Cormorants.

Shorebirds

Shorebirds are especially well known for their extensive migrations. Most species nest in the far north and winter in southern South America. In Maine this group is represented almost entirely by migrants — only 7 out of the 36 species that occur in Maine nest here. Migration continues almost throughout the summer. Spring migration begins in late April and extends through early June, peaking in mid-to-late May. Fall migration begins in early July and continues well into the fall, peaking between mid-August and early September. Since many prebreeding birds summer south of the nesting grounds, though, it is not unusual to see some migrants even in late June or early July. As elsewhere along the coast the fall migration is far more pronounced than the spring.

Common species that pass through are Semipalmated and Black-bellied Plovers, Killdeer, Whimbrel, Greater and Lesser Yellowlegs, Spotted Sandpiper, Ruddy Turnstone, Northern and Red Phalaropes, Short-billed Dowitcher, Semipalmated and Least Sandpipers, and Dunlin. Species regularly reported in small numbers are Piping Plover, Lesser Golden Plover, Upland and Solitary Sandpipers, Willet, Red Knot, Pectoral Sandpiper, White-rumped Sandpiper, Long-billed Dowitcher, Stilt and Western Sandpipers, Hudsonian Godwit, and Wilson's Phalarope. Please remember that shorebirds depend heavily upon traditional feeding and roosting grounds and are easily disturbed. Along many parts of the coast birds have already been forced into suboptimal habitats. PLEASE MAKE EVERY EFFORT NOT TO DISTURB BIRDS, especially when they're roosting.

Hawks

Compared with other parts of the east coast, hawk migration in Maine has received relatively little attention, and our knowledge of it reflects the localized nature of the coverage. Spring migration extends from about mid-April into May, generally peaking around April 20, while fall migration extends from early September through October, peaking around October 20. Fall migration is far more spectacular than spring for sheer numbers.

Accipiters and falcons, which are not as dependant as buteos on thermals, are the most common species on the coast. Sharp-shinned Hawks, American Kestrels, and Broad-winged Hawks are unquestionably the most abundant species, followed by Red-tailed Hawks, Merlins, Osprey, and Northern Harriers. Other species regularly reported in small numbers are Northern Goshawk,

Cooper's Hawk, Peregrine Falcon, and Red-shouldered and Rough-legged Hawks. The highest reported raptor counts usually come from Harpswell Neck near Brunswick. Other areas on or near the coast which afford good hawk-watching are Mount Agamenticus in the extreme southwest, Bald Rock Mountain in Camden Hills State Park, and Cadillac Mountain on Mount Desert Island.

Landbirds

Landbird migration, which includes several groups of birds, is very extended. Spring migration begins as early as mid-March, when Red-winged Blackbirds and Common Grackles appear, and continues through late May or early June when the last of the warblers pass through. In general, though, most landbirds pass through between late April and late May, with warblers peaking in the latter half of May. Fall migration may begin as early as mid-August and continue through October, without as pronounced a peak as in spring. Most birds on the coast in the fall are young birds, many of which get swept off course and land on offshore islands or the tips of peninsulas. This is one reason that strays and vagrants are seen most often in fall. Conditions for migration usually are best on a clear night with southwest winds in spring and northwest winds in fall. Many landbirds migrate at night, when they are less vulnerable to predators, and rest and feed by day.

Planning Your Trip

Weather

Mainers will tell you that they have two seasons, July and winter. There's an element of truth to that, but don't let it scare you off. (After all, many people here actually *like* the weather!) The average January temperature is 24° F; the average July temperature 67° F;

and the average annual snowfall 70 to 100 inches. But those are just averages. If there's one thing you can expect of Maine weather, it's the unexpected. Generally speaking, though, the weather from May through October usually is quite pleasant; from November through at least February bitter cold. Remember that in any season, and especially in winter, strong winds along the coast often make it feel colder than the thermometer reads. Fog is characteristic of the coast, and the farther east you go the more of it you'll see.

Tides

A tidal day lasts 24 hours and 50 minutes, and includes 2 low and 2 high tides. The average difference between high and low tide in Portland is 9 feet and in Eastport 20 feet. Each month there are two unusually high (spring) tides on the new and full moons and two unusually low (neap) tides on the quarter moons. Local papers carry tide tables.

Ferries

Many ferries offer good birding opportunities. Some of these, such as Isle au Haut or Monhegan, are mentioned in individual chapters, but many are not (Isleboro, North Haven, Vinalhaven, Matinicus, Swan's Island). Local chambers of commerce can provide schedules.

Clothes, etc.

In the summer you'll want warm-weather clothes such as T-shirts, shorts, and sandals, but you'll also want a heavy sweater, long pants, and warmer footwear. In winter bring the warmest clothes you have — thermal underwear, heavy wool socks, down parka, wool hat, mittens and scarf, and warm boots. FROSTBITE IS NO JOKING MATTER. We speak from experience. At any time of year bring a windbreaker and, especially if you plan to make any pelagic trips, raingear and waterproof boots.

You may want to bring some insect repellent for mosquitos and blackflies in summer. In winter make sure your car has lots of antifreeze and a strong battery.

Accommodations

Motels are easy to find along Route 1 from Kittery to Belfast. Farther east they are a bit scarce. Most are open only during the tourist season, late May through September. Campgrounds also are easy to find. In Appendix F you will find a partial list.

Note to the Reader

This book almost certainly will be revised in the future, and when it is it will be the better for your feedback. If you have any corrections or suggestions on how we can improve this book, please let us know. We'll be grateful for your help.

Finally, it is always with some concern that anyone shares their favorite birding spots with others, even in a book like this where many of the sites are well known. We do so with the fervent plea that wherever you bird you will keep the health of the environment and the welfare of the birds foremost in mind.

Southern
Coast

Chapter 1

Wells

The town of Wells, 20 miles north of Kittery, is a good place to see shorebirds, wading birds, and waterbirds. Characterized by extensive salt marsh, sand beach, and a protected harbor, much of the town shoreline lies within the Rachel Carson National Wildlife Refuge, a string of nine preserves which stretches from Kittery to Cape Elizabeth. Established in 1970 to protect long neglected and often abused wetlands, the refuge protects more than 750 acres in Wells, where coastal development has taken a particularly heavy toll. The deciduous habitat around Wells is a good area to look for several species of landbirds which approach the northern extent of their breeding range in southern Maine. Though generally not as productive a birding spot as Biddeford Pool or Scarborough Marsh to the north, Wells certainly warrants a visit. The focal points for birding are the Webhannet River marsh between Route 1 and Wells Beach; the Little River marsh and associated upland forest off Route 9E to the north; and Wells Beach and Harbor. There is good access to all these points from several roads running between Route 1 and the shore. The best of these, from south to north, are Mile Road, Lower Landing Road, Upper Landing Road, Drakes Island Road, and Route 9E. You can cover these areas in a few hours. Remember in the summer that Wells is overrun with people, so you may want to get here as early in the day as possible, especially if you want to walk the beach.

The best birding at Wells generally is the shorebirding. Common species you can expect to see here include Semipalmated, Black-bellied, and Piping Plovers, Killdeer, Greater and Lesser Yellowlegs, Short-billed Dowitcher, Sanderling, Semipalmated, Least, and Pectoral Sandpipers, and Dunlin (primarily fall). Less common species sometimes seen here are Solitary Sandpiper, Willet, and Wilson's Phalarope and, almost exclusively during fall migration, Hudsonian Godwit, Whimbrel, Long-billed Dowitcher, Red Knot, and Western, White-rumped, and Stilt Sandpipers. Though uncommon, as many as 10 Stilt Sandpipers have been reported here at once.

In the spring and summer Great Blue Herons, Green Herons, Snowy Egrets, Black-crowned Night Herons, and Glossy Ibises are regular in Wells, and occasionally a Little Blue Heron, Cattle Egret, Great Egret, or Louisiana Heron is also seen. Bonaparte's Gulls generally are common in spring and from mid-summer well into fall. Throughout the summer look for occasional Laughing Gulls, for Common and perhaps a few Arctic Terns, and for Little Terns and Piping Plovers which sometimes nest in small numbers on Drakes Island or Wells Beach. Offshore look for Common Eiders and Black Guillemots and around the marsh for nesting Sharp-tailed and Savannah Sparrows.

During spring and fall migration on the Webhannet and Little Rivers you may see Canada and sometimes Snow Geese (both species are more common in spring), American Black Ducks (year-round), Mallards, Blue-winged and Green-winged Teal, and Red-breasted and Common Mergansers. Occasionally you may also see Common Pintails, Ring-necked Ducks, American Wigeons, and perhaps a Gadwall or Northern Shoveler. Offshore look all winter for loons and grebes, Great Cormorants, and common sea ducks.

Thick-billed and Thin-billed Murres have also been seen off Wells in winter. Around the marsh in winter look for Snowy and Short-eared Owls, Rough-legged Hawk, Northern Shrike, and mixed flocks of Horned Larks, Snow Buntings, and sometimes Lapland Longspurs. In the harbor look over the gulls that congregate there, especially when a fishing boat comes in, for a Glaucous or an Iceland Gull.

A number of interesting landbirds can be seen around Wells. The White Pine forest off Route 9E is a good place to look for nesting Pine Warblers in the summer. Prairie Warblers are summer residents near the Wells dump, and in 1980 a pair of Louisiana Waterthrushes nesting along the Merriland River provided a first state breeding record (along with another pair of birds in Sweden). The deciduous habitat around these two areas, like other parts of Wells, is a good place to look for such species as Great Crested Flycatcher, Eastern Pewee, Wood Thrush, Veery, Red-eyed Vireo, Ovenbird, Scarlet Tanager, and Rose-breasted Grosbeak. Purple Martins nest in Wells and can often be seen over the marsh between Mile Road and Lower Landing Road.

A possible sighting of a Yellow Rail in the fall of 1976 is one of the most intriguing — if unconfirmed — records that Wells has yielded.

Directions

To reach Wells take Exit 2 off the Maine Turnpike. At the head of the exit turn left onto Route 9E/109S and continue 1.6 miles to the intersection with Route 1.

Mile Road lies 1.3 miles south of the Route 9/109 intersection on Route 1 and is well marked by a sign for Wells Beach. This road affords an excellent overview to the north and the south of the Webhannet River and Marsh. Follow the road to the end, stopping to scan along the way. At the shore is a large parking lot with access to Wells Beach. As you come out of the lot, turn right almost immediately onto Atlantic Avenue and drive 1.3 miles to the end for an overview of Wells Harbor. You'll see Lower Landing to the west, Drakes Island to the north, and open ocean to the east.

Lower Landing Road is probably the most productive birding spot in Wells, at least for shorebirds. At the intersection of Route 9/109 and Route 1, go north on Route 1 and then turn east immediately onto Lower Landing. In 0.4 miles you'll see the Webhannet Marsh on either side of the road, and 0.6 miles beyond this you'll see Wells Harbor.

Upper Landing Road comes out at the northern end of Webhannet Marsh. From the Route 9/109 and Route 1 intersection, go 0.9 miles north on Route 1 and turn right onto Upper Landing. This takes you right into the marsh, with another good perspective from which to scan.

Drakes Island Road is 1.1 miles north of the Route 9/109 and Route 1 intersection on Route 1. Follow the road 1.3 miles to a T-intersection, at which point you can go straight ahead to a small parking lot on the beach or turn right. (Turning left takes you down a dead-end with a "Private Property" and "No Parking" sign.) If you go right, bear left at the fork and continue to a parking lot overlooking Wells Harbor from the north. This is another good point from which to scan the harbor and open water.

Route 9E is 1.8 miles north of the Route 9/109 intersection with Route 1. Bear right onto it, following signs for Kennebunkport, and in 0.7 miles on your right you will see the entrance to the Rachel Carson National Wildlife Refuge headquarters. A trail here loops about 1 mile through the upland White Pine forest along the Little River and opens onto an extensive salt marsh with an overview of a barrier beach and beyond it open ocean.

Merriland River At the intersection of Route 9E/109S and Route 1,

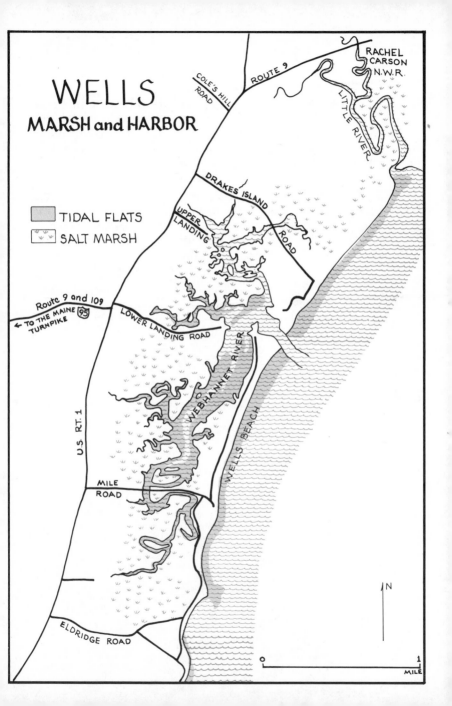

go north 1.5 miles and turn left onto Cole's Hill Road. In 1 mile you'll see the bridge over the Merriland River, and just before the river, on your right, is a path. Follow this past the rocky gorge to the lower and quieter section of the river. You can sometimes find Louisiana Waterthrushes here.

Wells Dump Turn right onto Route 9W at the head of Exit 2. Continue 2.1 miles (stay left at the fork) to the intersection with the Swamp John Road (unmarked), about 0.3 miles past the dump entrance. Prairie Warblers are heard and seen in the woods near the intersection regularly during the nesting season.

Accommodations
Motels are plentiful in Wells, though most are open only during the tourist season. There are four campgrounds in Wells.

Chapter 2

Biddeford Pool, Fletcher Neck and Wood Island

Biddeford Pool and Fletcher Neck offer some of the finest birding in Maine. Distinguished by a vast enclosed tidal pool and by an eastern arm that extends well into open ocean, this area provides a variety of habitats for shorebirds, wading birds, and ducks. It is an ideal stop-over for migrant landbirds and storm-tossed vagrants and is also a fine vantage point from which to scan for seabirds. Although it's particularly good for shorebirds on spring and fall migration, the area is also known as an exceptionally productive place where just about anything can turn up at any time of year —and often does. A Variegated Flycatcher in November of 1977 provided a first North American record, and a Rufous-necked Stint in July of the same year provided a first state record. Other unusual species seen here in recent years include Black Vulture, Gyrfalcon, American Oystercatcher, Curlew Sandpiper, Franklin's Gull, Royal Tern, Fork-tailed Flycatcher, Green-tailed Towhee, and

Black-headed Grosbeak. This area is well worth a visit at any time of year. Allow at least half a day to cover the area adequately, and in the summer avoid weekends if you want to see more birds than people.

Biddeford Pool

Biddeford Pool is a shallow basin that measures roughly 1 mile in diameter and empties into the sea through a narrow channel at its northeast corner. It is an excellent place to see a variety of shorebirds and wading birds. Bird it on a rising or falling tide, but not at high or low tide. Feeding generally is most fervid on the falling tide, since the high tide has replenished the food supply and the birds have not fed for several hours. Bear in mind that the pool tends to fill early — and the higher the tide, the earlier it fills. Depending on the height of the tide, the pool can be full anywhere from one to three hours before high tide. (If you're unfamiliar with the tides here, perhaps the best thing to do is to arrive well before high tide and bird Fletcher Neck first. That way you can come back to check the pool at regular intervals and catch it at just the right time. It is well worth the effort.)

The best way to bird the pool is to work the southern shore, from east to west on a falling tide and from west to east on a rising tide. The best access to the shore is by Hattie's Deli on the left side of the road, 1 mile after you turn left off Route 208 onto Fletcher Neck (park in the public beach parking lot, directly across from Hattie's). Behind the deli is a path which has been used by birders for years. This is private property, so ask inside before you go tramping out there. This path brings you out onto the pool's easternmost flats, which are the last flats to be covered on a rising tide and the first to be exposed on a falling tide. Large numbers of shorebirds congregate here on either side of the full tide and can be studied at close range. Please take care not to flush birds here, especially on a rising tide when they may be settling down to roost.

Common species that you can expect to see at Biddeford Pool include Semipalmated and Black-bellied Plovers, Killdeer, Greater and Lesser Yellowlegs, Spotted Sandpiper, Ruddy Turnstone, Short-billed Dowitcher, Least and Semipalmated Sandpipers, and Dunlin (primarily fall). Less common species are Willet and Pectoral Sandpiper and, in fall, Lesser Golden Plover, Hudsonian Godwit, Whimbrel, Red Knot, and White-rumped Sandpiper. Long-billed Dowitcher and Western Sandpiper aren't reported very often but probably are regular in small numbers. Marbled Godwit is rare but has been seen here.

In spring and summer Great Blue Herons, Green Herons, Snowy Egrets, Black-crowned Night Herons, and Glossy Ibises are regular around the pool, and occasionally a Little Blue Heron, Cattle Egret (as many as 21 on one occasion), Great Egret, or Louisiana Heron is seen. Laughing Gulls occasionally are seen in summer, and Bonaparte's Gulls generally are common in spring and from mid-summer well into fall. Sharp-tailed and Savannah Sparrows nest around the pool, and House Finches are year-round residents in the area.

In late summer and fall Forster's Terns have been seen around the pool, and Western Kingbirds are occasional then. The grasses and shrubs around the deli are a good place to look for migrating sparrows and other songbirds and from November through March for Horned Larks, Snow Buntings, and perhaps a Lapland Longspur. Where open water remains in winter you'll probably see American Black Ducks, Buffleheads, and Common Goldeneyes. Gulls often roost on the ice, and if you look them over carefully you may find a Glaucous or an Iceland Gull.

Fletcher Neck

From the pool follow Main Street around to the right and out onto Ocean Avenue on Fletcher Neck where you can park and scan the water. During the summer this is a good place to see Common Eiders, often with ducklings, Black Guillemots, and Arctic and Common Terns, all of which nest offshore. You should also look over Beach Island, directly offshore, for Roseate Terns. This is one of the few places in Maine where this species nests. From November through March look for loons, grebes, Great Cormorants, and common ducks and on the rocks for Purple Sandpipers.

East Point is the most productive birding area on Fletcher

Neck. The 30-acre sanctuary here is owned by the Maine Audubon Society and is accessible by a path that skirts the golf course. If you park at the north end of the oceanfront, where Main Street runs into Ocean Avenue, the entrance lies about 20 yards back on Main Street, marked by a chain link fence and, inside, a small Maine Audubon sign. Follow the path out to East Point and then west along the shore, which is heavily vegetated with Rugosa Rose, Bayberry, and Red Raspberry.

East Point is an excellent spot during migration to see a variety of warblers, including Orange-crowned in the fall, sparrows, and sometimes hawks, including Peregrine Falcon and Merlin. Plovers and sandpipers often roost at high tide on the rocks at the end of the point and on the pebbly beaches below the path on the north side of the neck. (Again, make every effort not to disturb roosting birds!) The golf course is as good a place as any to look in fall for Lesser Golden Plovers and for Baird's and Buff-breasted Sandpipers or in winter for a Rough-legged Hawk, Snowy or Short-eared Owl, or Northern Shrike. Swallows hawk overhead throughout the summer, and Gray Catbirds and Yellow Warblers nest in the shrubs around the point. Bank Swallows nest in the bank at the end of the point. From November through March scan for loons and grebes, ducks, gulls and alcids, and on the rocks Purple Sandpipers. A few Black-legged Kittiwakes, a King Eider, Harlequin Duck, and one or more alcids, including Thick-billed and Thin-billed Murres and Dovekies, are usually reported each winter. In spring you can sometimes see Brant here. With persistent scanning you may find a Northern Gannet at almost any time of year (except the dead of winter), and after a good strong easterly wind you might even see a shearwater, jaeger, or some other seabird normally not seen from the mainland.

From East Point continue south on the waterfront past the old Coast Guard station and around the loop at South Point, where you can scan the northern portion of Fortunes Rocks Beach, also good for shorebirds (Sanderling, plovers, "peep") and ducks. Some years Little Terns and Piping Plovers nest along this beach.

Another spot worth checking is the southern half of Fortunes Rocks Beach. From the west end of the pool go straight instead of turning right onto Route 208 to Biddeford. The next half mile of this road affords good views of the beach. It isn't an outstanding area by any means, but sometimes shorebirds roost here at high tide. If you miss the tide at the pool it's especially worth a look.

On your way back toward Biddeford explore the Hills Beach Road on the north side of the pool. It affords a good overview of the mouth of the Saco River and is a good place from which to scan for gulls and waterbirds, especially from November through March. From the pool head back toward Biddeford and take your first right off Route 208 onto Old Pool Road. Continue slightly more than 1 mile and fork right at the T-intersection onto Hills Beach Road. The road will dead-end at the northeast corner of the pool in about 1.5 miles. When you turn around, fork right at the T-intersection to get back on Route 208 toward Biddeford.

Wood Island

A half mile north of Fletcher Neck, and clearly visible from East Point, lies Wood Island. Owned by the Maine Audubon Society, the 42-acre island measures about 0.2 by 0.5 miles, with its long axis running east to west, and is densely vegetated with low shrubs and trees. A Coast Guard station stands on the east end of the island, and a boardwalk bisects the island from east to west.

Wood Island is one of only a few mixed heronries in Maine. Although numbers vary from year to year, the most recent survey found 28 pairs of Snowy Egrets, 21 pairs of Black-crowned Night Herons, 33 pairs of Glossy Ibises, and 1 pair of Little Blue Herons nesting here. Herring and Greater Black-backed Gulls and Common Eiders also nest on the island.

Because nesting waders are *extremely* vulnerable to disturbance, access to Wood Island is restricted during the breeding season. There is no public transportation to the island. Permission to visit the island must be obtained by writing or calling:

The Maine Audubon Society, Gilsland Farm, 118 Old Route 1, Falmouth, ME 04105   (207) 781-2330

If you do get permission to visit the island, you must keep to the boardwalk or the edge of the shore to avoid disturbing the birds.

Directions

To reach Biddeford Pool take the Maine Turnpike to Exit 5 and follow signs into Biddeford. At the first stop light in Biddeford cross Route 1 and immediately afterward turn right onto Main Street (Route 9). Cross the Saco River and take the soft left, not the hard left, onto Hill Street. Continue 0.3 miles and turn left at the stop light onto Pool Street (Route 9/208). Continue another 5.5 miles, bear left onto Route 208, and in 0.5 miles you'll see the pool on your left.

Accommodations

Motels are plentiful along Route 1 in southern Maine, though most are open only during the tourist season. There is a private campground in Biddeford.

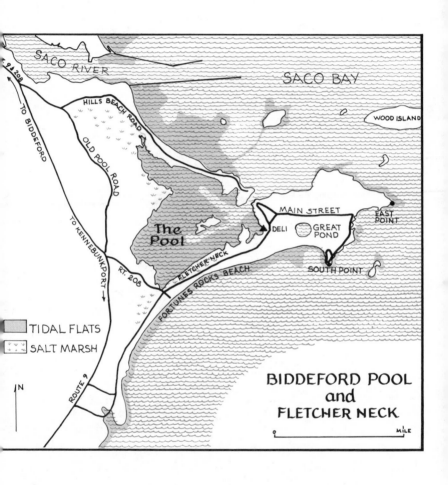

BIDDEFORD POOL
and
FLETCHER NECK

Chapter 3

Scarborough Marsh and Pine Point Narrows

The best place to see several species of wading birds in Maine and a good place to see a variety of migrating shorebirds and waterfowl is at Scarborough Marsh and Pine Point Narrows, about 10 miles south of Portland. Comprising nearly 3,000 acres traversed by five tidal rivers and several creeks and streams, the marsh is the largest salt marsh in the state. Within its extensive boundaries are an estimated 220 acres of mud flats, nearly 400 acres of brackish marsh, and 2,200 acres of salt meadow. Nearby at the mouth of the Scarboro River is Pine Point Narrows where there are extensive sand flats at low tide and good overviews of the Scarboro River and Saco Bay. Although both areas are well worth a visit at any time of year, birding generally is most productive from mid- or late March through November. Plan to spend a half day or so here.

Scarborough Marsh

Acre for acre the *Spartina* grass of a salt marsh produces more food for wildlife than any other natural habitat on earth. In spring and fall and throughout the summer, vast numbers of birds stop at Scarborough to feed and put on the fat that will fuel their long migrations. The Department of Inland Fisheries and Wildlife administers the marsh as a wildlife management area, and with their cooperation the Maine Audubon Society maintains the Scarborough Marsh Nature Center. Though very modest, it has an observation platform, a half-mile trail along the marsh on the other side of the road, and access to put in a canoe.

In March and April, when the marsh comes alive after a seemingly quiescent winter, large numbers of Canada Geese and smaller numbers of Snow Geese stop at Scarborough. Both species may be seen in the fall as well, but generally in smaller numbers. American Black Ducks, Mallards, Blue-winged and Green-winged Teal, and Red-breasted and Common Mergansers are also regular in spring as well as fall, while Common Pintails, Ring-necked Ducks, American Wigeons, Northern Shovelers, and Hooded Mergansers are occasional at those times.

In the summer Willets and Sharp-tailed and Savannah Sparrows nest in and around the marsh, and Great Blue Herons, Green Herons, Black-crowned Night Herons, Snowy Egrets, and Glossy Ibises come in to feed regularly. Occasionally a Little Blue Heron, Cattle Egret, Great Egret, or Louisiana Heron is also seen. Bonaparte's Gulls generally are common in spring and from midsummer into fall, while Laughing Gulls are occasional throughout the summer. Common Terns feed in the marsh in summer, as do small numbers of Little Terns, which nest on nearby Prout's Neck. Overhead look for an Osprey or a Northern Harrier.

In spring and fall, especially in the latter half of August, Scarborough Marsh is an excellent place to see an impressive variety of shorebirds. Regular species you can expect to see include Semipalmated and Black-bellied Plovers, Killdeer, Greater and Lesser Yellowlegs, Willet, Ruddy Turnstone, Short-billed Dowitcher, Semipalmated, Least, and Pectoral Sandpipers, and Dunlin (primarily fall). Less common species are Solitary Sandpiper and in fall Lesser Golden Plover, Hudsonian Godwit, Whimbrel, Long-billed Dowitcher, Red Knot, and Western, White-rumped, and Stilt Sandpipers. Marbled Godwit, Baird's Sandpiper, and Ruff are rare but have been seen here. Wilson's Phalarope is rarely reported but probably regular in small numbers. Look for it in shallow pools actively pursuing prey.

In winter Scarborough Marsh is a good place to look for a Rough-legged Hawk, Snowy Owl, or Northern Shrike. You should also look over the gulls that roost on the marsh for an Iceland or a Glaucous Gull. Horned Larks and Snow Buntings flock in the marsh grass, and sometimes you can find a Lapland Longspur among them. Where open water remains you'll see American Black Ducks, Buffleheads, Common Goldeneyes, and Red-breasted and Common Mergansers.

Among the most unusual species which have been seen at the marsh in recent years are Sandhill Crane, American Avocet, Caspian Tern, Northern Wheatear, and Loggerhead Shrike.

For another view of Scarborough Marsh drive down the Prout's Neck Road which lies just across the Scarboro River to the east (see next chapter).

Scarborough Marsh is open to the public year-round. Bear in mind, however, that it is a wildlife management area and not a refuge. In other words, trapping and duck hunting are allowed in season. (In southern Maine the duck season generally is split and runs from the beginning of October to mid-October and from mid-November through mid-December.) The Maine Audubon Society's Scarborough Marsh Nature Center is open in summer.

Pine Point Narrows

Just beyond Scarborough Marsh at the mouth of the Scarboro River the Pine Point peninsula stretches east toward Prout's Neck and forms the Pine Point Narrows. The protected basin that results is a good place to see a variety of waterbirds, and the extensive sand flats that are exposed at low tide make it an excellent shorebirding area.

From November through March check the narrows for loons and grebes and several species of sea and bay ducks. In summer

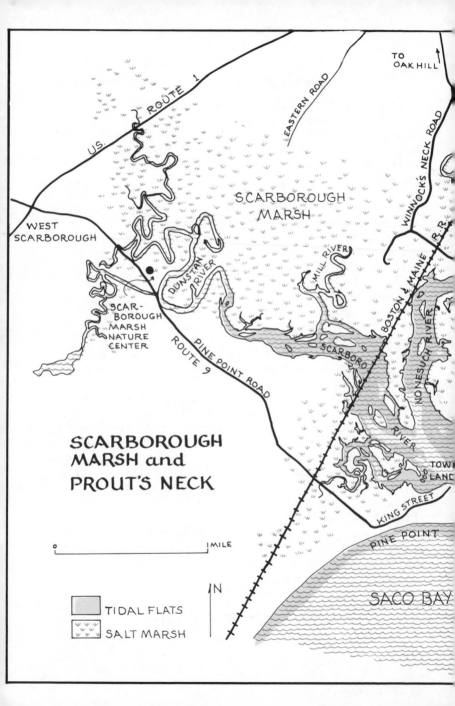

SCARBOROUGH
MARSH and
PROUT'S NECK

look for Little Terns and Piping Plovers, both of which nest on Prout's Neck some years, and in late summer for Forster's Terns, which have been seen here in small numbers on occasion. During spring and fall migration look for most of the same shorebirds that you'd expect to see at the marsh, as well as for Sanderlings. This is a good place to keep your eyes open for something unusual too. Pine Point Narrows provided Maine with its first two state records for Bar-tailed Godwit in August 1978 and 1980. American Avocet has also been seen here.

Directions

Coming from the south, take the Maine Turnpike to Exit 5. Follow signs for Saco-Biddeford, and in Biddeford turn north onto Route 1. Continue 6 miles to Route 9 (Pine Point Road) and turn right (east). You'll see the Scarborough Marsh Nature Center on your left in 0.8 miles. Coming from the north, take Route 295 through Portland and get off at the Scarborough-Old Orchard Beach exit. This will bring you onto Route 1, and from the intersection here Route 9 is 4 miles south. Turn left onto it.

To reach Pine Point Narrows continue 2.4 miles past the Scarborough Marsh Nature Center on Route 9, and instead of bearing right on Route 9 at the intersection here, continue straight through and turn left onto King Street. In about 0.5 miles King Street opens onto a municipal parking lot that overlooks the narrows. Coming back, turn left at the head of King Street and park at the beach where you can scan Saco Bay. You can get another overview of Pine Point Narrows from Ferry Beach on Prout's Neck (see next chapter).

Accommodations

There are plenty of motels along Route 1 in this area, though most are open only during the tourist season. There also are a few private campgrounds in Scarborough.

Chapter 4

Prout's Neck

Scarborough Beach State Park
Ferry Beach
Checkly Point

Another good birding spot about 10 miles south of Portland, and a good area to bird in conjunction with Scarborough Marsh, is Prout's Neck. Sticking like a fist into Saco Bay, Prout's Neck lies on the east side of the Scarboro River across from Scarborough Marsh and Pine Point. Former Prout's Neck resident Winslow Homer was inspired by the beauty of the coast here to create some of the world's most evocative and lovely seascapes. It is a fine place to see shorebirds and waterbirds and though there can be good birding all along the neck, the three main spots you will want to check are Scarborough Beach State Park, Ferry Beach, and the rocky tip of the neck at Checkly Point. Between them all you should find something of interest at any time of year. You can cover the area thoroughly in a few hours. By all means, though, avoid it entirely on summer weekends when it crawls with people.

Scarborough Beach State Park

Scarborough Beach State Park lies along the eastern shore of Prout's Neck. Its beach system measures an estimated 135 acres and includes a closed barrier beach that protects a freshwater marsh, with extensive stands of cattails, called Massacre Pond — so named because in 1713 twenty settlers were slaughtered here by Indians. Geologists speculate that perhaps 4,000 years ago this same beach system was an open barrier beach with a salt marsh and mudflats. As sea level has risen, the dunes have retreated up and over the old salt marsh, creating what you see today. There are a few low-relief parabolic dunes with healthy stands of American Beachgrass, a narrow band of dry, semi-open dunes, and good stands of Pitch Pine forest. The area is notable for the high diversity of its vegetational cover, which includes stands of the very fragile Beach Heather and patches of Earth Star Puffball and Tall Wormwood, which are uncommon in Maine.

The birds of Scarborough Beach are not particularly diverse, but the area is well worth a visit, especially in spring and winter. Oftentimes you can find a few specialties here that you might not see elsewhere. In winter, for example, this is a well known spot to see Harlequin Ducks, which are regular in small numbers offshore, and a King Eider or two among the large flocks of Common Eiders. Look also for loons and grebes, Great Cormorants, and common ducks. Sanderlings often linger well into winter, and you may see Purple Sandpipers fly by offshore. Look for Horned Larks, Snow Buntings, and perhaps a few Lapland Longspurs along the beach, and check the Pitch Pine and the shrubs around the pond for wintering passerines.

In spring look for Piping Plovers along the beach and for Marsh Wrens which nest among the cattails at Massacre Pond. You might find Pine Warblers resting in the Pitch Pines.

Scarborough Beach State Park is open year-round. In summer there is a small parking fee; in winter parking is free.

Ferry Beach

South of Scarborough Beach State Park and on the other side of Prout's Neck is Ferry Beach (also known as Western or Dollar

Beach) which overlooks Pine Point Narrows at the mouth of the Scarboro River. Ferry Beach comprises an area of about 27 acres, 22 of which are vegetated by dune plants, including Beach Heather and Tall Wormwood. Pine Point Narrows is formed by the convergence of Prout's Neck and Pine Point to the west and is notable for its extensive sand flats at low tide and its protected tidal basin. You can get another overview of the narrows from the end of Pine Point (see chapter 3).

In summer Little Terns and Piping Plovers sometimes nest along Ferry Beach, and Common, Arctic, and occasionally Roseate Terns feed offshore. Bonaparte's Gulls usually are common in spring and from mid-summer well into fall, and occasionally you may see a few Laughing Gulls. In late summer it's worth looking for Forster's Terns. From November through March look offshore for loons and grebes, Great Cormorants, and a variety of sea and bay ducks. In spring you can sometimes see Brant here. Check the beach in winter too, looking especially for a Lapland Longspur among the Horned Larks and Snow Buntings.

Checkly Point

Checkly Point is the southwest tip of Prout's Neck and from October through March is a good place to see waterbirds and waterfowl. Harlequin Ducks are usually seen in small numbers each winter, and occasionally a King Eider or an alcid. It's also a good place to look for Purple Sandpipers. In summer look for Common Eiders, Common, Arctic, and Roseate Terns, and Black Guillemots. With careful scanning you may be able to find a Northern Gannet offshore at any time of year except the dead of winter.

There are a few other spots worth mentioning en route to Prout's Neck. The first of these is Winnock's Neck Road which forks right off Prout's Neck road 0.6 miles south of Route 1. Follow this road around to the left and down to the railroad tracks that cut across Scarborough Marsh. There are small pools here that attract shorebirds and wading birds.

Another good place worth visiting is the marsh on either side of Prout's Neck road 0.8 miles south of Route 1. In spring you often see Snowy Egrets and Glossy Ibises here and occasionally a Green Heron or Black-crowned Night Heron. It's also a notably reliable spot to see Pectoral and Solitary Sandpipers and nesting Sharp-tailed Sparrows. Half a mile or so south you'll see another stretch of marsh which is also worth scanning. Check both these spots in winter for a Snowy or Short-eared Owl or a Rough-legged Hawk.

Directions   *(See map on pages 42-43.)*

To reach Prout's Neck traveling from the south, take the Maine Turnpike to Exit 5. Follow signs for Saco-Biddeford, and in Biddeford turn north onto Route 1. The Prout's Neck road — Route 207 or Black Point Road — is slightly less than 9 miles ahead. Turn right (east) onto it. Coming from the north, take Route 295 through Portland and get off at the Scarborough-Old Orchard Beach exit. This will merge with Route 1. Continue 1 mile south to Route 207 and turn left.

Scarborough Beach State Park lies on the eastern side of Route 207, 4 miles south of Route 1. To reach Ferry Beach continue 0.3 miles further and turn right onto Ferry Road. (There is a hefty parking fee here in summer.) Checkly Point is 1 mile south of Ferry Beach on Route 207.

Accommodations

Motels are plentiful on Route 1, though most are open only during the tourist season. There are a few private campgrounds in Scarborough.

Chapter 5

Portland

Back Cove
Mackworth Island Causeway
Maine State Pier and
    Eastern Promenade
Evergreen Cemetery
Route 95 Flats and Marshes

With a population of about 62,000, Portland is the largest of Maine's cities. Largely situated on a saddle-shaped peninsula that extends into Casco Bay, the city is surrounded on three sides by the bay, Back Cove, and the Fore River. Its deep sheltered harbor has made it an important seaport since its settlement in the seventeenth century, and today Portland is a major crude oil port on the east coast. Though hardly a wilderness area, Portland offers some fine birding.

Back Cove
The best birding in Portland is right in the heart of the city at Back Cove. Established as a wild bird sanctuary in 1915 and administered by the Department of Inland Fisheries and Wildlife, this shallow bay measures slightly less than 1 mile in diameter and includes some 33 acres of tidal flats. Along its eastern shore runs

Route 295, while Baxter Boulevard circles it on the west. If nothing else it's certainly one of the most convenient birding spots around, and it usually has something good to offer at any time of the year. Back Cove is a fine place to see ducks in fall, winter, and spring, shorebirds on spring and fall migration, and gulls year-round. It also attracts a few rare or unusual birds each year with surprising regularity. Whistling Swan, American Oystercatcher, American Avocet, Black-headed Gull, Little Gull, Forster's Tern, Black Skimmer, Yellow-headed Blackbird, and Seaside Sparrow have been seen here in recent years. It's a well-known spot to see Barrow's Goldeneye and Iceland and Glaucous Gulls in winter and Upland Sandpiper in spring and fall.

You can scan Back Cove from anywhere along Baxter Boulevard. The best way to bird the area, though, is from the parking lot along the southeast shore. Exit Route 295 in Portland at Forest Avenue North (Route 100), take your first right at the light onto Baxter Boulevard, and then take your first right again. You'll see the parking lot ahead on your left. If you park here you have direct access to the shore as well as to the weedy field between the east shore and the interstate. This field is a good birding spot in itself, so be sure and scan it carefully, as well as the cove and the shore. For another view of the cove, simply get back on Baxter Boulevard and circle around to the west and the north.

From early October through March Back Cove is an excellent area for duckwatching. You're likely to see large numbers of American Black Ducks, Buffleheads, and Common Goldeneyes, as well as Mallards, Red-breasted Mergansers, Greater and Lesser Scaup (the former more likely), and sometimes Common Pintails (most likely in early fall and spring). Also look for Barrow's Goldeneye which is regular here in small numbers each winter. As many as 23 have been seen at one time. Herring, Greater Black-backed, and Ring-billed Gulls roost along the shore all year (the last in smaller numbers in winter). Look for a Black-headed Gull among them, especially in fall or early winter, and for a Glaucous or an Iceland Gull from November through March. The field between the shore and the interstate is a good place to see a Snowy

Owl in winter and to look for a Lapland Longspur among the Horned Larks and Snow Buntings that often flock there.

In the summer regular species at Back Cove include Double-crested Cormorant, Great Blue Heron, Snowy Egret, Black-crowned Night Heron, American Black Duck, Blue-winged and Green-winged Teal (early and late summer), and Common Tern. Glossy Ibises are occasionally seen in spring. Bonaparte's Gulls are common in spring and from mid-summer into fall, and Laughing Gulls are occasional throughout the summer. In late summer it's worth looking for a few Forster's Terns, which have been seen here in small numbers.

During migration shorebirds roost along the eastern shore of Back Cove at the edge of the field. The most abundant species, which vary according to season, usually are Black-bellied Plovers, Greater and Lesser Yellowlegs, and Dunlin (primarily fall). Semipalmated Plovers, Ruddy Turnstones, Least and Semipalmated Sandpipers, and Short-billed Dowitchers are also common, though, and Pectoral Sandpipers are occasional. It's always worth looking for a White-rumped Sandpiper or in fall for a Lesser Golden Plover, Western Sandpiper, Long-billed Dowitcher, or Hudsonian Godwit, all of which can be seen here. Black-bellied Plovers and Dunlin often linger well into December. In spring and fall Upland Sandpipers are regular in the field, with as many as 11 birds having been seen here at once. The birds are well camouflaged, though, so the best thing to do is to walk through the grass and try to flush one. Listen in spring for their slurred, wolf-whistle-like call, rising sharply then trailing off gradually.

You should also check the inlet to Back Cove, especially in winter, on the other side of Route 295. From Forest Avenue get back on Route 295 North and in about 1 mile start looking on the east side of the interstate, where the Tukey Bridge crosses the mouth of the cove, for the inlet by the Burnham and Morrill baked bean factory. Pull off to the right here just after you cross the bridge, and scan the gulls which congregate at the sewage outlet. This is a good place to see a Glaucous or an Iceland Gull or even a Black-headed Gull in winter and Laughing Gulls in summer.

Mackworth Island Causeway

If you're in the vicinity of Back Cove on a cold winter's day there are a few other spots you should check, especially if you still haven't seen a Barrow's Goldeneye or a white-winged gull. One of these is the Mackworth Island Causeway in Falmouth. Coming from Portland take the Falmouth Foreside exit, just north of Back Cove, off Route 95 onto Route 1 and cross the Presumpscot River. Continue 0.2 miles and turn right onto Andrews Avenue, which leads onto the causeway.

This is a good spot to see many common waterbirds, but the highlight is Barrow's Goldeneye which regularly winters here in small numbers. Look for it among flocks of the much more numerous Common Goldeneyes. If you don't see it here, try walking the path that goes around the perimeter of the island. There is a small parking lot on your left immediately after you cross the causeway onto Mackworth Island, and the path begins here. This also makes a nice walk at the height of spring or fall migration.

Maine State Pier and Eastern Promenade

The other place you should check near Back Cove, from November through March, is the Maine State Pier on Commercial Street. Thousands of gulls often roost here, and you'll rarely have a better opportunity to study immature and winter-plumage gulls any closer. Herring and Greater Black-backed Gulls are by far the most abundant species, with smaller numbers of Ring-billed and sometimes Bonaparte's Gulls (primarily spring and fall) also present. This is an excellent spot to look for Glaucous and Iceland Gulls. If you don't find large concentrations of gulls here, investigate the many other piers along the waterfront.

To reach the Maine State Pier, take the Franklin Street exit off Route 295 in Portland. In less than 1 mile Franklin Street runs into Commercial Street at the waterfront, and the Maine State Pier lies directly ahead where you see the big blue warehouse. There is a sign which says that this is private property; ask someone on the grounds or inside the warehouse for permission to park and bird.

Coming back out of the Maine State Pier, jog right and continue north on Fore Street, which swings around onto Eastern Promenade. This historic drive affords a panoramic view of Casco Bay and is another good place from which to scan for loons, grebes, ducks, and gulls. Eastern Promenade brings you out on Washington Avenue. Turn right onto Washington to get back on Route 295.

Evergreen Cemetery

Evergreen Cemetery on Stevens Avenue is a good place to see a variety of warblers on spring and fall migration right within the heart of Portland. The municipal cemetery includes 370 acres of mixed deciduous trees with some conifers and many shrubs. The best birding generally is in the back of the cemetery where there are four small ponds.

The spring warbler migration usually peaks in Portland about the second week in May, while the fall migration is best in the latter half of August. You're likely to see all of Maine's regular migrant warblers here, with a good chance of something unusual too. Worm-eating Warbler is the rarest species that's been seen here in recent years. Be sure to be here early in the morning.

A Fish Crow seen here in recent years is among the few state records for this species.

To reach the cemetery, exit Route 295 in Portland at Forest Avenue North (Route 100). From the first light, at the intersection of Forest Avenue and Baxter Boulevard, continue 0.8 miles to Woodfords Corner where five streets meet. Take the soft left, not the hard left, onto Woodfords Street and continue 0.5 miles. Turn right onto Stevens Avenue, and you'll see the cemetery on your left in 0.5 miles.

Route 95 Flats and Marshes

On Route 95 from the north side of Portland to Yarmouth there are several good vantage points overlooking Casco Bay to the east and salt marshes to the west. These areas are often well worth a scan. At low tide the flats on Casco Bay are a good place to see large numbers of shorebirds in spring and fall and large numbers of gulls at any time of the year. It's another good spot to look for white-winged gulls. In spring and fall look for ducks and geese, including Snow Geese. The marshes on the west side of the interstate are also good for gulls and shorebirds and occasionally for wading birds.

Directions

To reach Portland from the south, exit the Maine Turnpike at Exit 6A and follow signs for Route 295 into the city. From the north, simply follow Route 95/295 into the city.

Accommodations

Motels, hotels, and inns are abundant in and around Portland. There are private campgrounds nearby in Westbrook to the south and Freeport to the north.

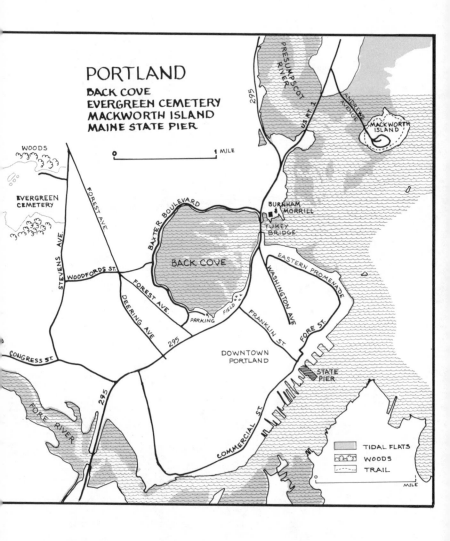

PORTLAND
BACK COVE
EVERGREEN CEMETERY
MACKWORTH ISLAND
MAINE STATE PIER

WOODS

EVERGREEN CEMETERY

PRESUMPSCOT RIVER

295

US RT 1

ANDREWS AVENUE

MACKWORTH ISLAND

0   1 MILE

FOREST AVE

STEVENS AVE.

BAXTER BOULEVARD

BURNHAM MORRILL

TUKEY BRIDGE

WOODFORDS ST.

FOREST AVE.

BACK COVE

EASTERN PROMENADE

DEERING AVE.

PARKING   FIELD

FRANKLIN ST.

WASHINGTON AVE.

FORE ST.

295

CONGRESS ST.

DOWNTOWN PORTLAND

STATE PIER

COMMERCIAL ST.

295

FORE RIVER

TIDAL FLATS
WOODS
TRAIL

0   MILE

Mid-Coast

Chapter 6

Brunswick Region

Bailey Island
Harpswell Neck
Brunswick Railroad Tracks
New Meadows River

Some good landbirding on Casco Bay can be had in and around the town of Brunswick, 26 miles north of Portland on Route 1. With its access to several peninsulas and its variety of habitat this area offers consistently good birding, particularly during migration. The town also is home to Bowdoin College which for many years has been known for its ornithology studies. You may be interested in visiting the A.O. Gross Library of Ornithology at Bowdoin, which can be arranged by calling Charles E. Huntington, Professor of Ornithology at the college.

The birding spots described below are the best in the area. You can cover them all in a half day or so.

Bailey Island

All the islands and peninsulas in Casco Bay, from Cape Elizabeth on the west to Cape Small on the east, offer some fine migration birding. We think the best of them is Bailey Island. The last in a series of three islands which are connected by bridge with the mainland in Brunswick, Bailey Island sticks further out into Casco Bay than any other point that can be reached by car. It is a fine stop-over point for migrants and wind-blown vagrants and is a good place to look for seabirds and a variety of landbirds on spring and fall migration. It is well worth a visit at any time of year.

Bailey Island measures about 2 miles by 0.5 miles and has many year-round and summer homes. Almost all of the island is private property, but at the peak of migration you can do some fine birding along the road. The best policy is to walk the road and, if you see some place you want to go, stop a passerby or knock and ask. Chances are you'll be welcome.

Drive to Land's End at the end of Bailey Island where you can park and scan. Species that nest on Casco Bay islands and are commonly seen from here include Double-crested Cormorant, Great Blue Heron, Snowy Egret, Black-crowned Night Heron, Common Eider, Osprey, Common and Arctic Terns, and Black Guillemot. In winter you'll see a good variety of common water-birds here, and possibly Purple Sandpipers. Look especially for an occasional King Eider among the large flocks of Common Eiders and for alcids, the most likely being Black Guillemot. With careful scanning you may find a Northern Gannet far offshore at almost any time of year except the dead of winter. After a good strong easterly wind we've even seen Sooty and Manx Shearwaters here. Brant are occasionally seen in spring.

After you've scanned Land's End, walk the road back north for a half mile or so and bird the shrubby roadside edge habitat. The shrubs around the parking lot at Land's End can be particularly productive. During migration (second and third weeks in May and any time from late August into October) this is a good place to look for a variety of common coastal migrants, particularly warblers. It is also a good place to look for vagrants. Among the most unusual species which have been seen on or from Land's End in recent years are Gyrfalcon, Willow Ptarmigan, Black-headed Gull, White-eyed Vireo, and Hooded Warbler.

Other areas to check on Bailey Island are Washington Avenue

on the east side of the island 0.7 miles north of Land's End (good water views and good roadside shrub habitat) and the field at Mackerel Cove 1 mile north of Land's End on the west (sometimes good for sparrows). One last place you should check is a prominent rise on Orr's Island, 1.6 miles after you cross the bridge from Bailey Island onto Orr's Island, which offers a commanding view up and down Harpswell Neck to the west. This can be an excellent vantage point for hawkwatching, particularly for accipiters and falcons. The Casco Bay area has long been known as one of the best fall hawkwatching spots in Maine.

Harpswell Neck

West of Bailey Island, Harpswell Neck stretches 10 miles into Casco Bay and like Bailey Island also offers some fine migration birding. Here again, though, most of the area is private property and you have to work the roadsides.

Drive to Pott's Point at the end of Harpswell Neck, where you can scan for waterbirds and seabirds year-round. There's a parking lot by Estes' Lobster House where you can leave your car. From here work the roadside during spring and fall migration to look for landbirds.

Another spot worth checking on Harpswell Neck is the Dolphin Marina on Basin Point. Although this is private property, birders are welcome. (If you're smart you'll fieldcheck the restaurant for blueberry muffins first.) The fields around the Dolphin and the last 2 miles of road that lead into it offer much the same birding as the end of Bailey Island. This area also is particularly good for fall hawkwatching, and the mudflats at Basin Cove (between the marina and Route 123) are worth checking for shorebirds.

An alternative to driving straight back to Brunswick is to return by way of Pennellville. This is a beautiful area of large open hay fields just south of Brunswick. The extensive fields here are good for a variety of open-country birds. The suggested short side loop is a very pleasant drive and offers a view of all the fields in the area.

From the West Harpswell School, continue 9.2 miles north

on Route 123 to Dyer's Corner. Turn left onto Middle Bay Road and left again onto Pennellville Road in 0.4 miles. Follow this until the paved road swings sharply right onto Pennell Way. Continue to the T-intersection, turn right onto Simpson's Point Road and then eventually right again onto Merepoint Road. This will lead you back to Maine Street in Brunswick.

Bobolinks and Eastern Meadowlarks nest in these fields. Watch the phone wires and fence lines for these two species as well as for American Kestrel and Eastern Kingbird. Swallows, including Cliff and Barn, can be seen coursing over the grass. During migration such birds as Cattle Egret, Glossy Ibis, Upland Sandpiper, Black-bellied Plover, and Water Pipit stop occasionally in the fields. In fall look for Western Kingbird and Loggerhead Shrike on the wires and for large flocks of sparrows along the roadsides. Red-shouldered Hawk and Northern Goshawk nest in the extensive White Pine and mixed deciduous woods surrounding the fields and are frequently seen overhead, the latter species being resident year-round. On a warm spring night in May you may hear Barred and Saw-whet Owls, American Woodcock, and Whip-poor-wills calling around the fields.

Brunswick Railroad Tracks

One of the more obscure birding spots around Brunswick is along the railroad tracks right in the center of town. On an early morning in May, though, this is a fine place to see spring warblers. At the height of migration you might see 18 to 20 species in an hour or so, and on an exceptional morning even more.

The stretch of tracks to walk is behind the Stowe House (so named for Harriet Beecher Stowe, who wrote *Uncle Tom's Cabin* here), an inn and restaurant on Federal Street. The left-hand (north-bound) track is good only for about 200 yards, while the right-hand (east-bound) track is good for half a mile or so and generally is more productive.

Spring migration here peaks in the second or third week of May, and if you are here early enough (no later than 7:00 A.M.) you can expect to see a good number of migrants.

New Meadows River

One last spot you should check, at least in late fall and early spring when there is open water, is the New Meadows River on Route 1 between Brunswick and Bath. Stop by the bridge and scan for Barrow's Goldeneyes and Hooded Mergansers, both of which are usually seen here in small numbers each year at these times.

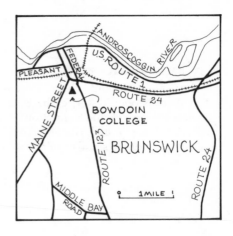

Directions

Bailey Island. Exit Route 1 east of Brunswick at Cook's Corner. Go straight at the head of the exit onto Route 24 and drive almost 18 miles to Land's End.

Harpswell Neck. From the center of Brunswick follow Maine Street south and at the top of the hill, just beyond the First Parish Church, turn left. At the first stop light turn right onto the Harpswell Road (Route 123) and continue 13.5 miles to Pott's Point. (Coming from Bailey Island, drive 7.1 miles north from Land's End and turn left onto Longreach Mountain Road. Continue 2.6 miles to Route 123 and turn left. Pott's Point is 7.3 miles south.)

    To reach the Dolphin Marina, drive 2 miles north from Pott's Point, turn left at the West Harpswell School, and follow signs to the Dolphin.

Brunswick Railroad Tracks. From the center of Brunswick follow Maine Street south and at the top of the hill, just beyond the First Parish Church, turn left. At the first stop light turn left onto Federal Street and in 0.2 miles right onto Maple Street. Maple Street winds around to the right, and you will see the tracks ahead of you.

Accommodations

There are several motels in Brunswick. The nearest campgrounds are on Orr's Island and in Freeport.

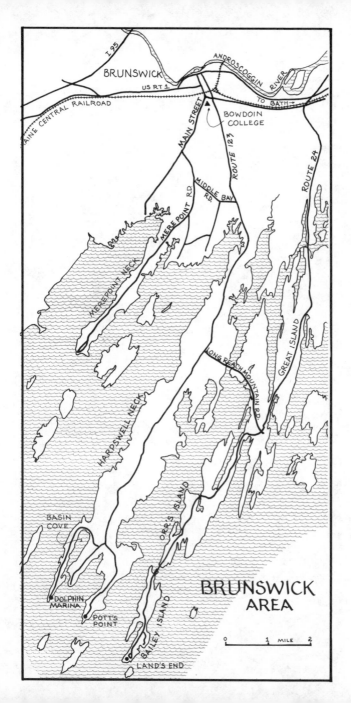

Chapter 7

Merrymeeting Bay and Bath Golf Club

Merrymeeting Bay

One of the best places in Maine to see large numbers and a good variety of waterfowl is northeast of Brunswick on Merrymeeting Bay. Called "Merrymeeting" by early English explorers because it was a rendezvous point for several Indian tribes, the bay is formed by the confluence of two major rivers — the Kennebec flowing in at the north and the Androscoggin at the southwest — and three lesser rivers: the Muddy, the Cathance, and the Abagadasset. About 5 miles long and varying from 0.5 to 3 miles wide, the bay comprises 4,500 acres of prime duck habitat. At the mouths of the rivers are broad and fertile mudflats which are exposed at low tide and produce lush growths of important food and cover plants, while at high tide the flooded flats provide extensive feeding and resting grounds. American Black Ducks, Blue-winged Teal, and Wood Ducks nest along the bay, and another 12 waterfowl species regularly stop over on migration. The bay also provides nesting habitat for 1 pair of Bald Eagles and is the most reliable place in

Maine south of Mount Desert Island for seeing this species. The best time to see waterfowl is from late March, when the ice goes out, through April and from early September through at least October. The best time to see eagles is in the winter. Allow about half a day to drive around the bay at the height of migration.

Regular waterfowl migrants on Merrymeeting Bay include enormous numbers of Canada Geese (primarily spring, peaking mid-April), smaller yet sometimes substantial numbers of Snow Geese (primarily spring) and American Black Ducks, and good numbers of Mallards (particularly fall), Common Pintails (particularly fall, when they are very early migrants), Green-winged and Blue-winged Teal (particularly early fall), Wood Ducks, Ring-necked Ducks, Greater and Lesser Scaup, Common Goldeneyes, Buffleheads, Common Mergansers, and to a lesser extent Red-breasted Mergansers. Gadwalls, American Wigeons, and Hooded Mergansers are occasional on the bay and usually more likely in fall. Pied-billed Grebes, Common Gallinules, and American Coot are also seen on the bay at times, especially in shallow waters close to shore. Rare migrants on the bay have included Whistling Swan, Fulvous Whistling Duck, Eurasian Wigeon, Northern Shoveler, Redhead, Canvasback, and Ruddy Duck.

In the Kennebec River above Merrymeeting Bay lies Swan Island, a rectangular island about 4 miles long and less than 1 mile wide. The island's name presumably derives from the Indian word *swango*, meaning eagle, and to this day 1 pair of Bald Eagles still nests here. Although at one time as many as 15 pairs of eagles nested around the bay, this is now the only one. Swan Island is open for camping from May through August, and although the area where the eagles nest is restricted, you can see it on a special tour given by the Department of Inland Fisheries and Wildlife. Aside from the Swan Island birds, the most reliable time to see eagles on the bay is from November through March when several birds, mostly subadults, winter here. With careful scanning you can sometimes see 1 or 2 birds on a drive around the bay at that time of year.

Merrymeeting Bay covers an extensive area, and most of the property that surrounds it is privately owned. The best way to bird the area is to drive a loop around it, up the west side from Topsham to Richmond, where you cross the Kennebec, and back down the east side to Bath. Generally the west side is more productive than the east. You'll see most of the bay this way, and at a few spots you'll get good overviews of large portions of the bay. In addition to good birding on the bay itself, this loop leads you through a variety of upland habitats, including coniferous (mostly White Pine) and deciduous woods, alder swales, fields, and scrub, with a good diversity of landbirds to be found. These habitats are all worth checking from spring migration through summer and fall. Some of the regularly seen or heard breeding landbirds include Northern Goshawk, Red-shouldered Hawk, Ruffed Grouse, Great Horned Owl, Whip-poor-will, Pileated Woodpecker, Great Crested Flycatcher, Phoebe, Eastern Pewee, Cliff, Tree, Bank, Barn, and Rough-winged (Muddy River bridge) Swallows, Gray Catbird, Brown Thrasher, Wood and Hermit Thrushes, Cedar Waxwing, Red-eyed Vireo, Yellow, Canada, and Chestnut-sided Warblers, Ovenbird, American Redstart, Northern Oriole, Scarlet Tanager, Rose-breasted Grosbeak, Purple Finch, Rufous-sided Towhee, Indigo Bunting, and Field, Chipping, and Song Sparrows. In April and September you'll often see several species of migrating hawks as you drive around the bay. In winter check the fields for Snowy Owls, the field borders for Northern Goshawk, Barred Owl, Northern Shrike, and Tree Sparrows, and look and listen for such winter visitors as Pine Grosbeak, Pine Siskin, Evening Grosbeak, Common Redpoll, and Red and White-winged Crossbills. Along the way, the Topsham dump provides a good opportunity to see Northern Ravens and raptors, including Northern Goshawk.

Merrymeeting Bay is a wildlife management area administered by the Department of Inland Fisheries and Wildlife. Bear in mind that it is a popular duck hunting area. In southern Maine the duck season is usually split, running from early October to mid-October and from mid-November through mid-December. For reservations or further information about Swan Island, write:

Wildlife Division, Department of Inland Fisheries and Wildlife, 284 State Street, Augusta, ME   04333

Directions

There's no easy way to give directions around Merrymeeting Bay. If you're not familiar with the area, by all means bring a map! As you drive the loop, though, you'll see that these directions really aren't as complicated as they seem.

Traveling from the north or the south, take Route 1 into Brunswick and follow signs for Topsham. Once you cross the Topsham bridge continue 0.3 miles to the second light and fork right onto Elm Street (Route 24). Proceed 0.7 miles and fork right again onto Foreside Road. In 2.5 miles you'll see the Topsham Dump on your left, and in another 1.4 miles you'll see Pleasant Point Road on your right. You can drive 1.2 miles down this road, which affords a lovely view of the bay, but after this the road is private so you must turn around. Back on the Foreside Road, continue north another 1.5 miles to the junction with Route 24. From this point you'll continue another 3.9 miles—traveling along a hilltop with a distant but sweeping view of the bay and through the town of Bowdoinham— and then you'll turn right (east) at the top of the hill onto Brown's Point Road. Brown's Point Road rejoins Route 24 in 4.4 miles, but just to confuse people, it's called Pork Point Road at this end. Turn right onto Route 24 again, continue 4.5 miles through Richmond and fork right onto Route 128, and continue 11.5 miles to the junction with Route 127. (The pond at the corner here is worth a look in spring and fall, particularly for Ring-necked Ducks.) Turn right onto Route 127, continue 2 miles to the junction with Route 1 in Woolwich, and turn right. The city of Bath lies just over the Kennebec.

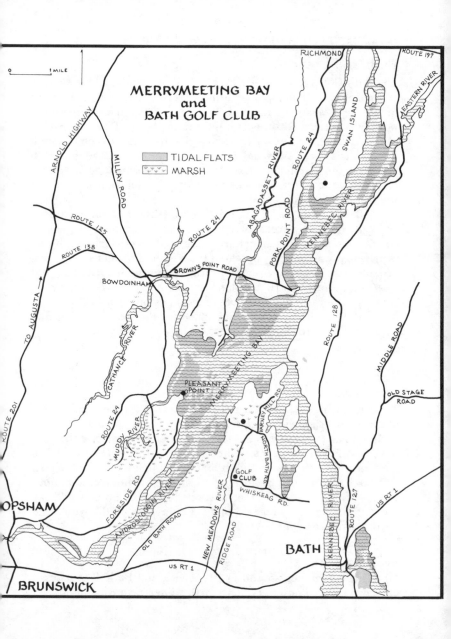

MERRYMEETING BAY
and
BATH GOLF CLUB

TIDAL FLATS
MARSH

0   1 MILE

RICHMOND
ROUTE 197
EASTERN RIVER
SWAN ISLAND
ROUTE 24
ABAGADASSET RIVER
PORK POINT ROAD
KENNEBEC RIVER
ARNOLD HIGHWAY
MILLAY ROAD
ROUTE 125
ROUTE 138
TO AUGUSTA
BOWDOINHAM
BROWN'S POINT ROAD
ROUTE 24
CATHRANCE RIVER
ROUTE 128
MIDDLE ROAD
OLD STAGE ROAD
PLEASANT POINT
MERRYMEETING BAY
ROUTE 201
ROUTE 24
MUDDY RIVER
BARNEY MILL RD.
NORTH BATH RD.
FORESIDE RD.
ANDROSCOGGIN RIVER
GOLF CLUB
WHISKEAG RD.
KENNEBEC RIVER
ROUTE 127
US RT 1
OPSHAM
OLD BATH ROAD
NEW MEADOWS RIVER
RIDGE ROAD
BATH
US RT 1
BRUNSWICK

Bath Golf Club

The Bath Golf Club in West Bath lies about 1 mile south of Merrymeeting Bay, flanking a beautiful freshwater marsh at the head of the New Meadows River. It is a notably reliable place to see nesting American Bitterns, Virginia Rails, Soras, Common Snipe, Marsh Wrens, and Swamp Sparrows. The best time to come is soon after sunrise on a May morning. As you approach the golf club you'll see the marsh just west of the club house. As long as you arrive before the golfers you can park along the roadside and explore the area.

If you don't see all these species at the golf club, explore some other nearby areas. A road runs north just west of the golf course, and along it is an extensive stand of cattails; although this is private property you can scan it from the road, and usually it's a reliable spot to see the wrens. If you continue another 0.4 miles and turn left, there's a small marsh on the north (right) side of the road where you can also see the wrens and usually both rails.

Most of the landbirds mentioned for the Merrymeeting Bay loop can also be found in this area.

Directions

To reach the Bath Golf Club, take Route 1 to West Bath and get off at the New Meadows Road/West Bath exit. Turn north at the head of the exit and continue to the stop sign; then jog right and then immediately left at a crooked intersection. In 0.8 miles the road takes a sharp right, and the golf club marsh lies just ahead on the left. Coming back, turn right, instead of left at this intersection, onto the road that runs north along a wooded ridge. In 1 mile you'll see the cattail stand on your left, and 0.4 miles beyond this you'll see the other road on your left.

Accommodations

Motels are open year-round in Brunswick and Bath. The nearest campground we know of is a KOA in Gardiner, near Richmond.

Chapter 8

Popham Beach State Park and Morse Mountain Preserve

Popham Beach State Park and Morse Mountain Preserve in Phippsburg offer some of the most consistently good birding along the
mid-coast. Located on opposite sides of the Morse River on Cape
Small, about 12 miles south of Bath, these adjacent areas include
two spectacular beach systems that together cover more than 1,000
acres and afford an excellent opportunity to see seabirds, waterfowl, migrating shorebirds, and some landbirds. Each area is well
worth a visit at any time of year. If you want to cover both areas
thoroughly, plan to spend close to a full day. While Popham Beach
is readily accessible, Morse Mountain is secluded, open to foot traffic only. It is a 2-mile hike to the beach.

Popham Beach State Park

With an estimated 618 acres of supratidal sand, Popham Beach is one of the largest and most complex beach systems in Maine. It is bounded on the west by the Morse River, a tidal inlet, and on the east by the Kennebec River. Popham Beach State Park is only the western half of this system; Hunnewell Beach and Coast Guard Beach constitute the eastern half. Within the state park's 554 acres are well over 1 mile of a wide beach face, a barrier dune field, associated salt marsh, and a spit and tidal inlet. At low tide extensive sand flats are exposed. Botanically the park supports unusually large stands of Beach Heather, the largest stands of American Beach Grass in Maine, and the largest mature Pitch Pine forest on sandy dunes in Maine.

The birding at Popham Beach State Park and the surrounding area is good year-round. The best way to cover the area is to park in the main parking lot and work a loop. Scan the beach and the tidal pools below the parking lot, walk or scan Hunnewell Beach to the east (far more developed and usually not as productive), and then walk west down Popham Beach to the Morse River. As you come back up from the river, look for a path, unmarked but well-trodden, that cuts behind the dunes and along the edge of the salt marsh. Follow this and you'll end up at a small parking lot 0.3 miles west of the main lot. Walk the road back to the main lot, scanning the marsh on the left side of the road as you go, and then work the Pitch Pine forest in the backdune and the shrubs around the foredunes and the parking lot.

In summer Popham Beach is a good place to look for Common, Arctic, and Roseate Terns. All 3 species nest on the Upper and Lower Sugarloaf Islands that you see at the mouth of the Kennebec. Double-crested Cormorants, Herring and Greater Black-backed Gulls, Common Eiders, and a few Black Guillemots nest on the 3 Heron Islands just south of the Morse River. Ospreys nest nearby and often are seen offshore, and Little Terns and Piping Plovers sometimes nest near the Morse River. Also look for Bonaparte's Gulls around the Morse River in spring and from midsummer well into fall and for an occasional Laughing Gull throughout the summer. Around the salt marsh look for nesting Sharp-tailed and Savannah Sparrows and for wading birds. Great Blue Herons, Green Herons, Snowy Egrets, and Black-crowned Night Herons are regular here, and occasionally you may see a Little Blue Heron, Great Egret, or Louisiana Heron. Check the Pitch Pines for nesting Pine Warblers.

During migration shorebirds feed on the sand flats offshore and along the Morse River. Regularly seen species include Semipalmated, Piping, and Black-bellied Plovers, Killdeer, Greater and Lesser Yellowlegs, Spotted Sandpiper (often nesting by the Morse River), Short-billed Dowitcher, Sanderling, Semipalmated and Least Sandpipers, and Dunlin (primarily fall). You're also likely to see a few Whimbrels or Willets here and occasionally a Hudsonian Godwit or Western, White-rumped, or Pectoral Sandpiper. Scan carefully for a Lesser Golden Plover, Long-billed Dowitcher, or Red Knot. (Except for Willet and Pectoral Sandpiper, these less common species are seen almost exclusively in fall.) Look offshore for migrating Northern Gannets and waterfowl (the latter particularly in fall), and keep your eyes open for migrating hawks as well. The path that cuts up along the marsh is an excellent place to look for migrating passerines, particularly sparrows and warblers, as are the Pitch Pine forest and the shrubs around the dunes and parking lots.

In winter, when finding birds anywhere in Maine gets tough, take a trip to Popham Beach to lift your spirits. Like Reid State Park on the other side of the Kennebec, Popham is a better place than most to see a good variety of species from November through March. And even if you don't see much, the winter beach is spectacular. Look offshore for loons and grebes, Great Cormorants, and common sea ducks. Common Pintails are occasional. Look also for an occasional King Eider or alcid and in early spring for Brant. Sanderlings are common along the beach usually through December, and a few Lapland Longspurs sometimes flock among the Horned Larks and Snow Buntings that are often here. Other species to look for on the beach or on and around the marsh are Rough-legged Hawk, Snowy Owl, Northern Shrike, and Common Redpoll. Check the Pitch Pine forest for Golden-crowned Kinglets and for such irregular winter visitors as Pine Grosbeaks, Pine Siskins, and Red and White-winged Crossbills. Rarities seen at Popham Beach in recent years include Royal Tern and Brewer's Blackbird.

Two spots very near the state park are also worth checking.

Spirit Pond, at the head of the Morse River, is a good place to look for gulls and at mid- and low tide for shorebirds. Fort Popham at the mouth of the Kennebec is an excellent vantage point (better than the state park) from which to scan for terns on the Upper and Lower Sugarloaf Islands.

Popham Beach State Park is open year-round from 9:00 A.M. to sunset. There is a small parking fee in summer. In winter, when the park gate is usually closed, park outside and walk in. Bear in mind that in summer the park usually is very crowded, especially on the weekends.

Morse Mountain Preserve

Morse Mountain lies on the west side of the Morse River, adjacent to Popham Beach State Park, and is a private nature preserve and conservation area. Thanks to the extraordinary generosity of the St. John family and Bates College, birders and other nature enthusiasts may use the area. The preserve is open during daylight hours year-round to foot traffic only. It is a 2-mile hike from the parking lot to the beach. Unfortunately, the area has been abused recently, and restrictions may eventually make it inaccessible.

Habitats at Morse Mountain include extensive salt marsh, a hemlock-spruce-fir forest, a Pitch Pine forest, and an extensive beach system. Seawall Beach is the only large, unaltered barrier spit in Maine. Anchored to a rocky headland at the northeast end, the beach and backdune area extend well over 1 mile to the southwest and protect an extensive salt marsh and tidal river complex, covering nearly 400 acres. Botanically the beach is known for its extremely high diversity of dune species, including extensive stands of Beach Heather, and as the northernmost coastal dune habitat for Earth Star Puffball. It may be a long walk, but this beautiful hike across salt marsh, up and over wind-flagged Morse Mountain, and down to Seawall Beach below is well worth the effort.

The birding at Morse Mountain is similar to that at Popham Beach State Park, and you can expect to see many of the same species. If Morse Mountain has any advantage over Popham, it lies in its seclusion and more extensive and diverse habitat. You're likely to see more nesting species and more migrant landbirds, particularly warblers, at Morse Mountain than at Popham, and it also is a better place to look for more unusual boreal species such as Northern and Black-backed Three-toed Woodpeckers, Gray Jay, and Boreal Chickadee. Other regular summer residents here, particularly in the hemlock-spruce-fir forest, include Ruffed Grouse, Eastern Pewee, Red-breasted Nuthatch, Brown Creeper, Winter Wren, Golden-crowned Kinglet, Blackburnian Warbler, and Northern Junco. You're also more likely to find Little Terns and Piping Plovers nesting on Seawall Beach than on Popham Beach.

The accessibility of a place like Morse Mountain to so many people is a gift that few landowners make. Please remember that and make every effort to observe the few regulations on the preserve and to respect the privacy of the families that summer here.

Directions

To reach Popham Beach State Park or Morse Mountain take Route 1 to Bath and then Route 209S to Phippsburg. Coming from the south, exit Route 1 just *before* the Bath Business District exit and turn right onto Route 209S. Coming from the north, exit Route 1 at the Bath-Phippsburg exit; immediately turn left at the stop sign and left again at the next stop sign; then continue slightly more than 1.5 miles and turn left onto Route 209S. Popham Beach State Park is about 12 miles south of Bath on Route 209S and is well marked by signs along the way. To reach Morse Mountain, go straight onto Route 216S in Phippsburg when Route 209S takes a sharp left. Continue 0.8 miles and turn left onto a narrow paved driveway that is marked "Private." In half a mile you'll see signs for the preserve and a small parking area.

Spirit Pond is on Route 209S, 2.2 miles east of the intersection of Route 209S and Route 216S. Fort Popham also is on Route 209S, 1.4 miles beyond the main parking lot at the state park.

Accommodations

Motels are open year-round in Bath and Brunswick. There is a campground in Popham Beach and two on Small Point.

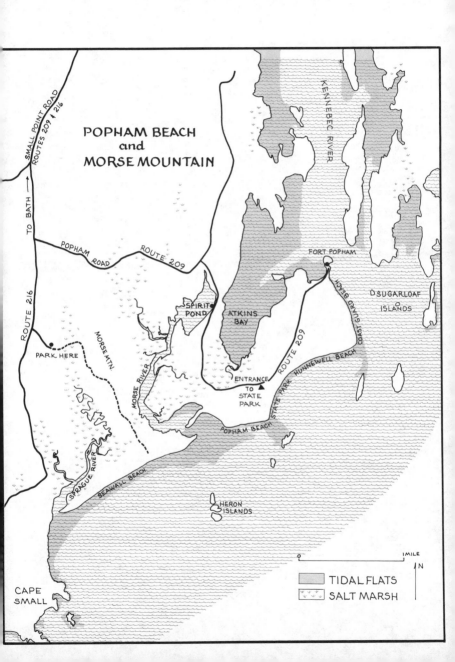

POPHAM BEACH
and
MORSE MOUNTAIN

SMALL POINT ROAD
ROUTES 209 & 216

TO BATH

POPHAM ROAD   ROUTE 209

ROUTE 216

MORSE MTN.

PARK HERE

MORSE RIVER

SPRAGUE RIVER

SEAWALL BEACH

CAPE SMALL

SPIRIT POND

ATKINS BAY

ENTRANCE
TO STATE
PARK

POPHAM BEACH STATE PARK

HERON ISLANDS

KENNEBEC RIVER

FORT POPHAM

SUGARLOAF ISLANDS

COAST GUARD BEACH

HUNNEWELL BEACH

ROUTE 209

1 MILE

N

TIDAL FLATS
SALT MARSH

Chapter 9

Reid State Park

Reid State Park in Georgetown is one of the loveliest spots along the Maine coast and a fine birding area. To many people, native and outlander alike, this is the quintessence of Maine — nearly 800 acres of coniferous and mixed deciduous woods, extensive salt marsh, rocky headlands, and more than 1.5 miles of sandy beach. Geologically the park is the northernmost large backdune habitat in the state, with an estimated 26.5 acres of dune and 35 acres of beach, and botanically it may be the northern range limit for several species, including Beach Heather and Jointweed. It is well worth a visit at any time of year. You can cover the park in less than half a day. Try to avoid it on summer weekends when it is very crowded.

The two most prominent features of Reid State Park are Mile Beach and Half Mile Beach. Mile Beach is a closed barrier beach that stretches from Griffith's Head — the bold rocky headland that dominates the park's northeast shore — southwest to Todd's Point, and behind it is a large salt marsh and salt water lagoon. Half Mile Beach is an open barrier spit that runs from Todd's Point west to a tidal inlet called the Little River, and it too protects a substantial salt marsh.

To reach the two beaches, take either of the park road forks just beyond the entrance gate. Bearing left takes you to the parking lot at Griffith's Head, with access to Mile Beach, while going straight takes you to the parking lot at Todd's Point with access to both beaches. From either lot, walk a loop around the beaches and the Todd's Point road. Both Griffith's Head and Todd's Point are good vantage points from which to scan. The Todd's Point road affords excellent overviews of the Mile and Half Mile beach systems, including the marshes and the lagoon, and is lined with coniferous and mixed deciduous woods that offer the most productive forest birding in the park.

In summer Reid State Park is a good place to see Common Eiders, summering scoters, Black Guillemots, and Common, Arctic, and occasionally Roseate Terns. Ospreys nest nearby at Robinhood Cove in Georgetown and are often seen offshore, and Little Terns and Piping Plovers sometimes nest on Half Mile Beach. Sharp-tailed Sparrows nest in the *Spartina* grass in the salt marshes, and Savannah Sparrows nest along the edges of the marshes. You can also see a variety of waders here, including Great Blue and Green Herons, Snowy Egrets, Black-crowned Night Herons, and occasionally a Little Blue Heron, Great Egret, or Louisiana Heron. Bonaparte's Gulls generally are common in spring and from mid-summer well into the fall, and Laughing Gulls are occasional in summer. The best place to look for gulls is at the Little River. In the woods along the Todd's Point road look and listen for Ruffed Grouse, Pileated Woodpecker, Olive-sided Flycatcher, Brown Creeper, and nesting warblers, including Magnolia, Black-throated Green, Blackburnian, and Pine. You're likely to hear a Northern Raven here at any time of year.

In spring and in late summer and fall check the Little River for shorebirds. The species diversity usually isn't too great here — nor are sheer numbers — but you never know what might turn up.

Semipalmated, Piping, and Black-bellied Plovers, Greater and Lesser Yellowlegs, Spotted Sandpiper (often nesting by the Little River), Ruddy Turnstone, Short-billed Dowitcher, Sanderling, Semipalmated and Least Sandpipers, and Dunlin (primarily fall) are regular. Look also for the occasional Hudsonian Godwit, Whimbrel, and Willet, and scan carefully for such species as Long-billed Dowitcher, Red Knot, and Western and White-rumped Sandpipers. Except for Willet, these less common species are seen primarily in fall. The most unusual species seen here in recent years was a single Baird's Sandpiper.

In spring and fall Reid State Park is a good place to look for migrating Northern Gannets offshore, for hawks, including Peregrine Falcons and Merlins, and for a variety of passerines, particularly sparrows, in the shrubs around the dunes and the parking lots. In the fall you can often see an impressive passage of waterfowl offshore, and in spring as well as fall you may see some interesting ducks on the lagoon behind Mile Beach.

From November through March, when Maine birding becomes a challenge by any standards, Reid State Park is a better place than most to see a good variety of species. In recent years it distinguished itself with a Western Grebe which was discovered on the 1977 Christmas Bird Count (for a first state record) and then reappeared dutifully for two more winters, lingering offshore several months each year. Scan from Griffith's Head and Todd's Point, where ducks and grebes tend to raft up, for Common and Red-throated Loons, Red-necked and Horned Grebes (the former being particularly abundant here most winters — a count of 185 in the winter of 1976-77 may have been a high for the northeast region), Great Cormorants, and a variety of common sea ducks. Common Pintails and Greater Scaup are occasional. This is a good place to look for a King Eider and for alcids. Black Guillemots are most likely, but Thin-billed and Thick-billed Murres and Dovekies have also been seen here. Purple Sandpipers are regular on the rocks all winter, and Sanderlings are common along the beaches usually through December. Look for dabbling ducks on the lagoon behind Mile Beach and for "Ipswich" Savannah Sparrows which winter in the dune grass. Lapland Longspurs sometimes flock among the Horned Larks and Snow Buntings on the beach, and at times a Snowy Owl is seen on the marsh. Look for Common Redpolls feeding on the ground or on birch catkins.

In the woods along Todd's Point road at this time of year look for Golden-crowned Kinglets and for such irregular winter visitors as Evening and Pine Grosbeaks, Pine Siskins, and Red and White-winged Crossbills. Northern Shrikes often perch on snags along the road here and on the edge of the marsh. Boreal Chickadees are regular in small numbers here each winter, and with a good Saw-whet Owl imitation and "pishing" you usually can call some up. Other unusual boreal species which have been seen here on rare occasions are Black-backed and Northern Three-toed Woodpeckers and Gray Jay. American Robins, Hermit Thrushes, and Yellow-rumped Warblers often linger through December, and it's always worth checking the shrubs around the dunes and parking lots for the odd passerine that winters over.

Finally, there are two spots you'll want to check en route to Reid State Park. The first is the Georgetown Post Office, 9 miles south of the intersection of Route 1 and Route 127 in Woolwich, where Hooded Mergansers are sometimes seen in early and late winter. Park by the small, gray shingled Post Office and scan the inlet from the bridge here. The other spot is a small pond 1.6 miles further south, on the right and just before you make a righthand turn, where Ring-necked Ducks are regular in spring and fall.

Reid State Park is open year-round from 9:00 A.M. until sunset. There is a modest parking fee. If you arrive early in the morning and the gate is locked, park outside and walk in.

Directions

To reach Reid State Park take Route 1 to Woolwich, which lies on the east side of the Kennebec across from Bath. At the stoplight on the east side of the Bath bridge, turn south onto Route 127. Continue 10.6 miles and turn right, following signs for the park, which lies 2.2 miles further.

Accommodations

Motels are open year-round in Bath. There are campgrounds on Small Point on the west side of the Kennebec.

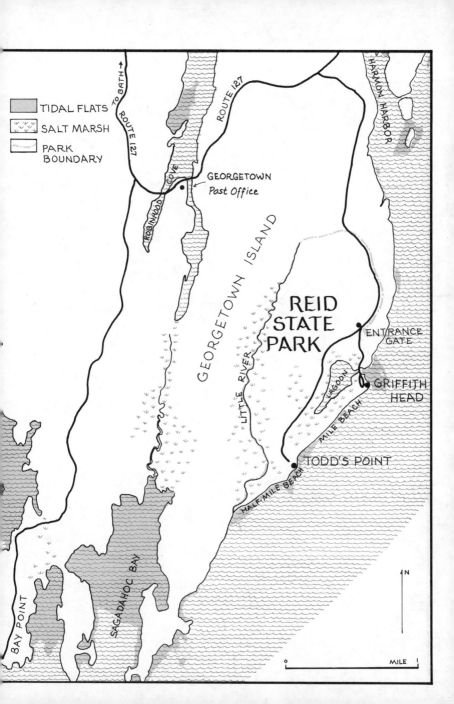

Chapter 10

Damariscotta Region

Sherman Lake
Damariscotta Mills
Pemaquid Point

The town of Damariscotta lies along the Damariscotta River and Route 1, midway between Bath and Rockland. The birding around this area is not exceptionally diverse, but the three areas mentioned here are places where you can often see specialties that are hard to find elsewhere. Sherman Lake is a good spot to see nesting freshwater marsh birds and migratory waterfowl, Damariscotta Mills is good for waterfowl and nesting Bald Eagles, and Pemaquid Point is an excellent vantage point from which to scan for seabirds year-round and for migratory landbirds. You can cover all three areas in a half day or less.

Sherman Lake

Sherman Lake lies along Route 1 midway between Wiscasset and Damariscotta. It is conveniently accessible from a highway rest stop and picnic area and from a side road that runs along the east side of the lake. The lake measures about 1 mile by 0.3 miles and is bordered by an extensive cattail marsh. An early morning in mid-May to mid-June is the best time to look for marsh birds.

Species you can expect to see at Sherman Lake are Pied-billed Grebe, Green Heron, American Bittern, Marsh Wren, and Swamp Sparrow. Keep your eyes open too for Least Bittern, a notoriously elusive species which has been seen here and may be nesting. American Black Ducks, Mallards, Blue-winged and Green-winged Teal, Ring-necked Ducks, American Coot, and other waterfowl are regularly seen here on migration and sometimes through the summer.

Damariscotta Mills

The crossroads of Damariscotta Mills lies on the upstream end of Salt Bay, a large (125-plus acres), shallow, estuarine portion of the Damariscotta River. A pair of Ospreys nests atop a power line pole on an island in the center of the bay, and waterfowl stop over here on spring and fall migration. From November through March, as long as there is open water, this is a reliable place to see Barrow's Goldeneyes and Hooded Mergansers, with as many as 100 of the latter having been seen here at once. A few Canvasbacks and Redheads are seen here some years too, and occasionally Pied-billed Grebes and American Coot are seen in spring and fall. The area you especially want to check is a small bridge across from a railroad embankment where there's usually open water most of the winter. If you don't see the birds here, drive a short way further on Route 215 North to another narrow bridge and look there. Gulls roost out on the ice in the bay in winter, and it's always worth checking them for a Glaucous or an Iceland Gull.

Damariscotta Mills also boasts a pair of nesting Bald Eagles. Because the nest was vandalized a few years ago, we hesitate to give directions to it, but the birds generally are on the nest by mid-February and sometimes can be seen over Salt Bay as they search for fish.

Pemaquid Point

Fifteen miles south of Damariscotta at the end of Pemaquid Neck is Pemaquid Point, a well-known and scenic promontory which many people know for its lighthouse and its vast expanse of rocks running seaward. Sitting well out in open ocean with a view of Monhegan Island to the south and overlooking Muscongus Bay from the west, it is a fine vantage point from which to scan for seabirds and waterfowl and a good place to look for migrant land-birds. At any time of year you're likely to see something of interest at Pemaquid Point, and this is particularly true after a good strong storm from the east. Sooty, Royal, and Sandwich Terns and Black Skimmer have been recorded in this area as storm-swept vagrants. The coniferous trees and shrubs around the point offer productive landbirding.

In spring and summer the lighthouse at Pemaquid Point is a good place from which to scan for Northern Gannets, Brant (spring), Common Eiders, Common, Arctic, and very occasionally Roseate Terns, and Black Guillemots. Bonaparte's Gulls generally are common in spring and after mid-July, and Laughing Gulls are occasional throughout the summer. From mid-June through at least August — with a scope and careful, persistent scanning — you can sometimes see Northern Fulmars, Greater, Sooty, and Manx Shearwaters, Wilson's Storm Petrels, Northern and Red Phalaropes (primarily late summer and early fall), and possibly a Parasitic or Pomarine Jaeger, Black-legged Kittiwake, or Atlantic Puffin from the point.

Just north of the lighthouse is a 1-mile loop road that is lined with coniferous trees and that affords more good overviews of open ocean. After you've scanned from the lighthouse, work this area. This is a good spot to look for migrating landbirds, par-ticularly warblers, and for nesting warblers throughout the sum-mer. Northern Ravens nest nearby and in recent years Red Crossbills have nested here. Watch for Olive-sided Flycatcher, Red-breasted Nuthatch, Brown Creeper, Winter Wren, and Golden-crowned Kinglet.

In winter Pemaquid Point is a better place than most to look for some hard-to-find species. Large numbers of Common Eiders raft offshore, and sometimes you can find a King Eider among them. Harlequin Ducks are occasional here, Black-legged Kittiwakes can be seen regularly (although as one local birder says, "you'll have to spend more than ten minutes looking for them"), and alcids often can be seen, especially on a calm day when they don't disappear among the waves. Look for Black Guillemots throughout the winter and for Thick-billed Murres, Razorbills, and Dovekies in early winter. This is also a good spot to see Purple Sandpipers. Check the loop road for crossbills and other winter finches.

One other spot on Pemaquid Neck that is worth checking, especially in winter, is Pemaquid Harbor. When the fishing boats come in they attract large numbers of gulls, including on occasion Glaucous and Iceland Gulls.

Directions

Traveling from the north or the south, take Route 1 to the Damariscotta area.

Sherman Lake, conspicuously marked by the rest stop, is on Route 1, 3.3 miles north of the Wiscasset bridge and 3 miles south of Damariscotta. The access road that runs along the east shore of the lake turns east off Route 1 0.6 miles north of the rest stop.

Damariscotta Mills lies just north of Damariscotta. To reach it coming from the south, get off Route 1 at the Damariscotta-Newcastle exit, follow the exit ramp down to the stop sign at Main Street, and go straight through the intersection onto Route 215 North. In 0.7 miles you'll see the edge of Salt Bay; in another 0.5 miles you'll see a spot on the right where you can pull off and scan the Osprey nest; and in 0.7 miles further you'll see the bridge by the railroad embankment on your right. If you continue another 0.4

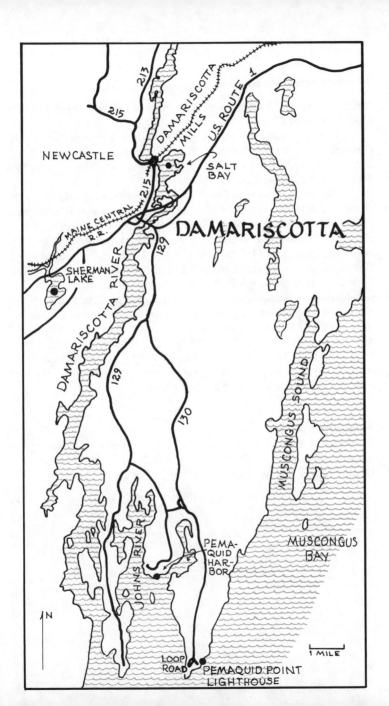

miles on Route 215 North, you'll see another narrow bridge that is also worth scanning.

Coming from the north, get off Route 1 at the Newcastle, Damariscotta, Damariscotta Mills exit and turn right onto Route 215 at the head of the exit. Continue 0.2 miles to the edge of Salt Bay and follow directions as above.

To reach Pemaquid Point, exit Route 1 from the north or the south as for Damariscotta Mills. Coming from the south, turn right at the stop sign on to Main Street, continue 0.4 miles, and fork right onto Route 129 South. In 2.9 miles fork left onto Route 130 South and continue 11.9 miles to the lighthouse at Pemaquid Point. Coming from the north, turn left at the head of the exit, continue 0.5 miles to the stop sign at Main Street, turn left, and follow directions as above. Coming out of the lighthouse parking lot, turn left almost immediately onto the paved loop road that comes back out on Route 130 in 1 mile. To reach Pemaquid Harbor, continue 2.4 miles north on Route 130 and turn left, following signs for Pemaquid Beach. In 1.2 miles go straight through a confusing four-corner intersection, and take your first right at Fort William Henry. The road leads down to the harbor.

Accommodations

There are motels and inns in Damariscotta and in neighboring towns. There is a private campground on Lake Pemaquid in Damariscotta and two more in nearby Nobleboro.

Chapter 11

Weskeag Marsh and Rockland Harbor

Weskeag Marsh

Weskeag Marsh in South Thomaston includes about 300 acres of salt, brackish, and freshwater marsh traversed by the Weskeag River and bordered by extensive hay fields and woodlands. Officially known as the R. Waldo Tyler Wildlife Preserve, the marsh is a wildlife management area administered by the Department of Inland Fisheries and Wildlife. It's a fine place to see nesting freshwater marsh birds, wading birds, migrant shorebirds, and some ducks. Though you'll rarely see large numbers of birds here, the variety usually is quite good. You can cover the area thoroughly in a few hours or less.

Weskeag Marsh is easily worked from Buttermilk Lane, which crosses and then parallels the Weskeag River. You can pull off the road and park by the culvert where the road crosses the river and then walk into the marsh on your right. (This is tough going, and if you have a canoe this is a good place to use it. A local birder tells us that if you put in at high tide you can make it down to the town landing and back before low tide. One word of caution: there's a tricky rip tide at the bridge in South Thomaston, so it's best not to go quite that far.) From the culvert continue up the ridge on Buttermilk Lane, where you have a distant but lovely overview of the marsh. You can pull off the road here too and walk down the hillside to the marsh below. In spring and summer check the cattail ponds on Buttermilk Lane and the Thomaston Road, and at any time of year check the Weskeag River from the town landing in South Thomaston.

In spring and summer look for Great Blue Herons, Green Herons, Snowy Egrets, Black-crowned Night Herons, Small numbers of Glossy Ibises, and an occasional Little Blue Heron, Cattle Egret, or Great Egret. Sharp-tailed and Swamp Sparrows nest here, and Northern Harriers, Osprey, and Common Terns feed here. Around the cattail ponds look for nesting American Bitterns, Soras, Marsh Wrens, and in some years Virginia Rails. Sedge Wrens also have nested here.

Common shorebirds you can expect to see on spring and fall migration at Weskeag include Semipalmated and Black-bellied Plovers, Killdeer, Greater and Lesser Yellowlegs, Short-billed Dowitcher, Semipalmated and Lesser Sandpipers, and Dunlin (fall). Look also for small but regular numbers of Whimbrels, Red Knots, White-rumped, Pectoral, and Stilt Sandpipers, and for an occasional Lesser Golden Plover, Solitary Sandpiper, Willet, Wilson's Phalarope, Long-billed Dowitcher, or Western Sandpiper. Most of these less common species are seen only during fall migration. In spring look for Upland Sandpipers in the fields along Buttermilk Lane and for Common Snipe and American Woodcock displaying in the fields adjacent to the marsh.

Common waterfowl migrants at Weskeag include Canada Geese, American Black Ducks, Mallards, Blue-winged and Green-winged Teal, and Red-breasted and Common Mergansers, while Common Pintails, Ring-necked Ducks, American Wigeons, Northern Shovelers, and Hooded Mergansers are occasional. Pied-billed Grebes and Common Gallinules are also seen on occasion.

In winter, like any extensive open area, Weskeag is a good

place to look for hawks and owls, particularly Rough-legged Hawk and Barred and Snowy Owls, and for Northern Shrikes, Common Redpolls, and mixed flocks of Snow Buntings, Horned Larks, and maybe Lapland Longspurs. At the town landing look for loons and grebes, Great Cormorants, ducks, and gulls. At any time of year you might see a Bald Eagle here.

Directions

Coming from the north or the south take Route 1 into Thomaston and just east of the huge Martin-Marietta Cement Plant turn south onto Buttermilk Lane — unmarked except for a small sign "To So. Thomaston." In 1 mile, where the road dips, you'll see the culvert and on your right Weskeag Marsh. If you continue another 0.4 miles you'll be atop the ridge that overlooks the marsh.

One of the cattail ponds you want to check is on Buttermilk Lane, 0.1 miles north of the culvert on the east side of the road; the other is 0.8 miles down the Thomaston Road which turns east off Buttermilk Lane 0.4 miles north of the culvert. This marsh is private property, but you can scan it from the road.

To reach the town landing in South Thomaston continue 1.4 miles south past the culvert on Buttermilk Lane, turn right, and proceed 1.1 miles.

Rockland Harbor

Situated at the southwest entrance of Penobscot Bay, the city of Rockland is an important fishing port and reputedly the largest lobster distribution center in the world. Its busy waterfront is known to birders as an excellent spot to look for gulls, particularly in winter.

At any time of year you can see Greater Black-backed, Herring, and Ring-billed Gulls in Rockland, and from November through March you often can find Glaucous and Iceland Gulls among them. Look also for Black-headed Gull, which is seen here on rare occasion. Bonaparte's Gulls can be seen year-round but are

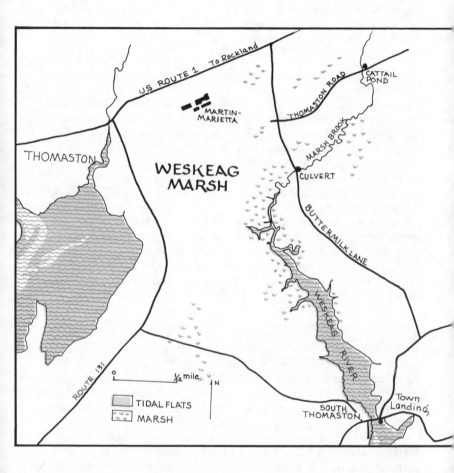

Little Tern, *Sterna albifrons*

Webhannet River and marsh, Wells

Lesser Yellowlegs, *Tringa flavipes*

Merrymeeting Bay

Path to Sieur de Monts Spring, Mount Desert Island

Purple Sandpipers, *Calidris maritima*

Schoodic Point

Quoddy Head State Park

Black-legged Kittiwake, *Rissa tridactyla*

Razorbill, *Alca torda*

Machias Seal Island, New Brunswick

Seawall Bog, Mount Desert Island

Moosehorn National Wildlife Refuge

Black-bellied Plover, *Pluvialis squatarola*

Greater Black-backed Gull, *Larus marinus*

Double-crested Cormorant, *Phalacrocorax auritus*

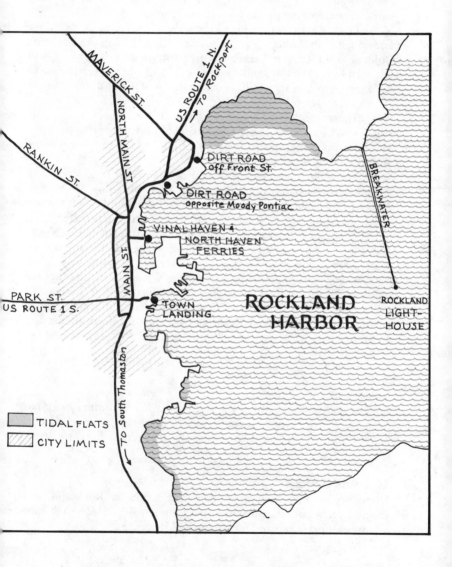

MAVERICK ST.

US ROUTE 1 N.
To Rockport

NORTH MAIN ST.

RANKIN ST.

BREAKWATER

DIRT ROAD
off Front St.

DIRT ROAD
opposite Moody Pontiac

VINAL HAVEN &
NORTH HAVEN
FERRIES

MAIN ST.

PARK ST.
US ROUTE 1 S.

ROCKLAND
HARBOR

ROCKLAND
LIGHT-
HOUSE

TOWN
LANDING

To South Thomaston

TIDAL FLATS
CITY LIMITS

most common in spring and from mid-July into fall, and Laughing Gulls are occasional throughout the summer.

Look also for wintering loons and grebes, Great Cormorants, and ducks, including an occasional King Eider or Barrow's Goldeneye, in Rockland Harbor. One winter a pair of Canvasbacks lingered here through January. If you take one of the ferries out of Rockland look for alcids, particularly Thick-billed Murres, Dovekies, and Black Guillemots.

There are several spots along the Rockland waterfront from which you can scan the harbor, and any of these is worth checking. The four stops mentioned below, though, are the most accessible and usually the most productive.

Working from the south end of Main Street to the north (Main Street is one-way going north), start by going down Park Street to the town landing. Scan here and then continue 0.3 miles north on Main Street to the Vinalhaven/North Haven ferry terminal. Scan both sides of the wharf here. Continue north on Route 1 and in 0.3 miles look for a narrow, unmarked dirt road on your right, across from Moody Pontiac. Drive just a short way down here, where you overlook the harbor. Finally, continue another 0.2 miles north on Route 1, fork right onto Front Street, and in 0.3 miles, where the road turns sharply to the left, go straight ahead down a dirt road to the shore. If you get back on Front Street and continue around the curve you'll intersect Main Street in 0.1 miles.

Directions

Traveling from the north or the south, take Route 1 into Rockland. From the south, Route 1 brings you into town right on Park Street. From the north, Route 1 intersects Park Street, where you turn left.

Accommodations

There are motels and inns open year-round in Rockland and Thomaston, a public campground at Camden Hills State Park, and private campgrounds in Thomaston and Rockport.

Chapter 12

Monhegan Island

Ten miles south of Port Clyde and well beyond Muscongus Bay lies one of Maine's most enchanting offshore islands — Monhegan. Called *Monahigan* by the Indians, meaning "island of the sea," Monhegan was a well-established settlement as long ago as 1622, and through the centuries it has held a special charm for people who have come to know it. For nearly a century it has been a favorite haunt of birders, and anyone who's birded here knows why: Monhegan has a reputation as Maine's finest "migrant trap" and annually attracts an astonishing variety of rare and uncommon species. Few if any other spots along the Maine coast can claim such a consistent list of rarities and vagrants, a list that in recent years has provided several first state records and has included Magnificent Frigatebird, Gyrfalcon, Rufous Hummingbird, Say's Phoebe, Carolina Wren, Northern Wheatear, Lazuli Bunting, LeConte's and Clay-colored Sparrows, and Lark Bunting, to name just some. The island is at its best during fall migration when it is known as one of the finest birding spots in the northeast, not only for its rarities but also for its concentrations of birds. By all means, though, visit Monhegan any time you have the opportunity — it almost always has something interesting to offer. Plan to spend two or three days, if you can, to do the island justice.

For a small, oval island that measures only 1.5 by 0.5 miles, Monhegan has a surprising variety of habitats. The island is bounded on the north and on the east by rocky headlands that rise to 160 feet, on the south by shallow, boulder-strewn coves, and on the west by the low-lying village. Spruces and firs blanket much of the interior, particularly on the north end of the island, while the southern end, which used to be farmed, is overgrown with Trailing Yew, alder swales, Shadbush, Chokecherry, and Rugosa Rose. There is a 2-acre ice pond at the north end of the village and a 20-acre swampy meadow in the village center. Seventeen miles of trails wind across the island, and visitors enjoy remarkable freedom to roam at will.

The most productive birding on Monhegan, at least for passerines, is around the ice pond and on the village road from the ice pond south to Lobster Cove. Along the way look at Swim Beach, the small cove just south of the Monhegan Store, for warblers feeding on the beach, especially in May. (We've actually handfed warblers, exhausted by migration, here.) Lobster Cove itself is fairly open and a good place to see migrating hawks and occasionally a few shorebirds. Look for seabirds, sea ducks, and Northern Ravens from the Cliff Trail on the east side of the island; for warblers on the Underhill, Burnthead, and Long Swamp trails; and for Brown Creepers, kinglets, nuthatches, Winter Wrens, and nesting warblers including Blackpoll in Cathedral Woods. On the north end of the island Green Point is an excellent vantage point from which to scan, especially at the height of fall migration when you can watch birds come in across the water. The ferry between Port Clyde and Monhegan also offers some fine birding.

Because of its offshore location, its remoteness (which means that there are no other islands on which birds can land), and its small size (which means that birds are more concentrated than they would be on a larger island), Monhegan is a particularly exciting place to be during migration. Spring migration usually reaches its peak about the third week in May, and at its height it is not at all uncommon to see between 75 and 100 species in a day. The highlight undoubtedly is the great variety of warblers. Fall migration, which is far more protracted, is good from the end of August through at least September. It offers an excellent opportunity to study immature and fall-plumage passerines and the best chance of seeing rarities and vagrants. While these may vary from year to year, species that have been seen on Monhegan include Yellow-crowned Night Heron, Yellow-billed Cuckoo, Western Kingbird, Blue-gray Gnatcatcher, White-eyed Vireo, Yellow-throated Vireo, Blue-winged, Orange-crowned, and Prairie Warblers, Yellow-breasted Chat, Yellow-headed Blackbird, Orchard Oriole, Blue Grosbeak, Dickcissel, and Lark Sparrow. Look for Red and White-winged Crossbills, which are notoriously erratic, at any time of year. Several species of hawks, including Merlins and Peregrine Falcons, can be seen on Monhegan during migration, and in fall you may see an impressive passage of waterfowl offshore. The meadow is a good place to look for migrating blackbirds and sparrows.

In summer Monhegan is a good place to see seabirds. Common Eiders, Herring and Greater Black-backed Gulls, and Black Guillemots nest on Eastern Duck Island north of Green Point. Other species you might see from Monhegan or from the ferry are Northern Fulmar, Greater, Sooty, Manx, and possibly Cory's Shearwaters, Wilson's Storm Petrel (all "tubenoses" primarily from mid-June through July), Northern Gannet, Osprey, Common and Arctic Terns, and Northern Phalaropes (primarily August and early September). Look also for an occasional Parasitic or Pomarine Jaeger, Black-legged Kittiwake, Atlantic Puffin, or Razorbill.

If you have a chance to visit Monhegan in winter, which is difficult to arrange with the inns closed, you'll find more good birding. If nothing else, you can at least take the ferry over and back in one day, though it doesn't give you any time to explore the island. From November through March look from Monhegan and from the ferry for Common and Red-throated Loons, Red-necked and Horned Grebes, Northern Gannet (with careful scanning sometimes seen in every month except January and February), Great Cormorant, and several common ducks. Occasionally you may see a King Eider or a Harlequin Duck. You should also see large numbers of Herring and Greater Black-backed Gulls, some Black-legged Kittiwakes, and possibly Iceland and Glaucous Gulls. Christmas Bird Count participants even turned up a Black-headed Gull one year. This is also a good opportunity to look for all 6 alcids. On Monhegan itself look especially for Purple Sandpipers along the rocky shores, for such species as Snowy Owl, Northern Shrike, Common Redpoll, Red and White-winged Crossbills, and Lapland Longspur, and for the odd passerine that winters over.

As if a preponderance of birds weren't enough, there is more to Monhegan's charm. The island offers quiet and lovely vistas, a long and fascinating history, a delightful simplicity of life, and comfortable accomodations. A single visit simply can't do justice to Monhegan or its birds.

Directions
Monhegan is served by ferry from Port Clyde, twice daily from June 20 through September 20 and once daily the rest of the year. The trip out takes about one hour. For a schedule write or call:

> Capt. James Barstow
> Monhegan-Thomaston Boat Line
> PO Box 238
> Port Clyde, ME 04855
> (207) 372-8848

To reach Port Clyde take Route 1 to Thomaston and on the east side of town turn south (by the huge, white Montpelier mansion) onto Route 131. Proceed 15 miles to Port Clyde. The dock is located to

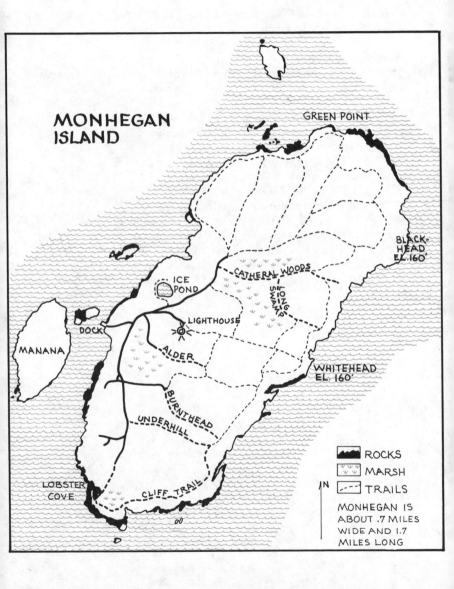

MONHEGAN
ISLAND

GREEN POINT

BLACK-
HEAD
EL.160'

CATHERAL WOODS

ICE
POND

SHOING
SWAMP

DOCK

LIGHTHOUSE

MANANA

ALDER

WHITEHEAD
EL.160'

BURNTHEAD

UNDERHILL

LOBSTER
COVE

CLIFF TRAIL

ROCKS

MARSH

N↑ TRAILS

MONHEGAN IS
ABOUT .7 MILES
WIDE AND 1.7
MILES LONG

the left of the Port Clyde General Store, and overnight parking is available there for a small fee.

Accommodations

There are three inns on Monhegan, all of which require reservations well in advance. Write:

> The Trailing Yew (open May 15 through October 15)
> Monhegan House (Memorial Day weekend through
>   September)
> The Island Inn (June 15 through September 15)
> Monhegan, ME 04852

There is no camping allowed on the island.

There are no winter accommodations on Monhegan, but occasionally island residents will rent rooms to visitors. The best bet is to ask the innkeepers if they know of anyone willing to do this.

There is no electricity on Monhegan, so be sure to bring a flashlight. You can get a good map of the island at the Monhegan Store.

Mount Desert Region

Chapter 13

Isle au Haut

When Samuel de Champlain sailed up the Maine coast in 1604 he called the outermost island in Penobscot Bay Isle au Haut. Rising abruptly from the sea, the "high island" of the famous French explorer has since come to be known as one of Maine's loveliest and most enchanting offshore islands. It is also a fine place to bird, particularly during spring and fall migration. Separated from the town of Stonington on Deer Isle by 6 miles of island-dotted waters, Isle au Haut is an outpost of Acadia National Park, whose boundaries encompass nearly half the island's 4,700 acres. Although it's possible to make a day trip, you'll want to spend at least one night, and preferably two or three, to see all that the island has to offer. The campground is open from mid-May through mid-October and provides the only accommodations. The best times to visit are in mid- to late May and from late August well into the fall, when the island is full of migrants.

Isle au Haut is among the largest of the many islands in outer Penobscot Bay, measuring 6 miles by 3 miles with its long axis running north-south. A ridge of hills runs the length of the island, and the highest of these, Mt. Champlain, rises to 543 feet. The island is boreal in character and except for small cultivated areas near habitations is heavily forested, primarily by spruces and firs. There are several swampy and marshy areas on the island, a number of small streams that drain the interior, and on the east side a large meadow and freshwater pond. The shore is uniformly rocky and rugged with several indentations and promontories. A small village lies on the north and east shores, and a 12-mile road loops around the island, though only 5 miles are paved and you'll rarely see a car outside the village. Thirty-odd miles of trails make virtually the entire island accessible to visitors.

Birding is at its best on Isle au Haut during the spring and fall migrations. Spring migration generally peaks about the third week in May, when breeding-plumage warblers are a specialty, while fall migration, which is far more protracted, is good anytime from late August through at least September. It's in late summer and fall that you're most likely to see rarities and routine vagrants such as southern and western strays. During either migration the best birding for passerines is around the Duck Harbor campground and around Turner Pond (also known as Long Pond) and Great Meadow on the east side of the island. The loop road, which provides a good edge habitat, also makes a fine birding trail and is well worth a round-trip hike. Also check the marsh at Merchant's Cove, where you'll often see species you won't see elsewhere on the island. Although the island isn't particularly good for shorebirds, this usually is the best place to see any. The south end of the island is the best place from which to scan for offshore species.

In the spring and summer on Isle au Haut look for such regular species, some of which breed on the island, as Red-breasted Nuthatch, Golden-crowned and Ruby-crowned Kinglets, Olive-sided, Yellow-bellied, and Least Flycatchers, Winter Wren, Hermit, Swainson's, and Gray-cheeked Thrushes, and a good variety of warblers including Tennessee, Magnolia, Cape May, Black-throated Blue, Bay-breasted, Blackpoll, Pine, Palm, Mourning, and

Wilson's, and Lincoln's Sparrow. On a spring evening listen for the hooting of a Great Horned Owl. On the south end of the island hike from Western Head to Eastern Head via the Cliff Trail and Goat Trail, which is spectacularly beautiful on a sunny day. Double-crested Cormorants, Common Eiders, Osprey, Greater Black-backed and Herring Gulls, Common and Arctic Terns, and Black Guillemots all nest offshore. Look also for Northern Gannets, Northern and Red Phalaropes (primarily late summer and fall), Bonaparte's and Laughing Gulls, and an occasional Black-legged Kittiwake. With good strong easterly winds and a little luck you might even see a "tubenose" or jaeger. In the coves look particularly for Harlequin Ducks, which winter regularly in large numbers off Isle au Haut and often linger into June. In May you might still see Purple Sandpipers in the coves too.

In the fall look for a variety of common coastal migrants on Isle au Haut and keep your eyes open for unusual offshore island species such as Western Kingbird, Yellow-throated Vireo, Yellow-breasted Chat, Orchard Oriole, Dickcissel, or Lark Sparrow. While Isle au Haut's larger size and proximity to so many other islands make it less of a "migrant trap" than Monhegan, it nonetheless offers some fine birding at this time of year.

At any time of year look for Boreal Chickadees, which nest some years on nearby Vinalhaven and are seen regularly on Isle au Haut. Northern Ravens are permanent residents on the island, and Red and White-winged Crossbills, which are very erratic, are another possibility at any time of year.

The winter ferry schedule unfortunately makes birding on Isle au Haut impossible from mid-October through mid-May (unless you know an island resident who'll put you up). At the very least, though, you can take the ferry over and back. Look for loons and grebes, Great Cormorants, ducks, gulls, including Glaucous and Iceland Gulls, and alcids. In March of 1979, 149-plus Harlequin Ducks seen at Isle au Haut may well have been the highest number ever recorded in the northeast in this century.

Directions

Isle au Haut is served by mailboat from the town of Stonington on Deer Isle, three times daily in summer and once daily in winter. The trip across takes about 45 minutes each way. A schedule is available from Acadia National Park in Bar Harbor. In summer a park ranger usually meets the ferry.

To reach Stonington take Route 1 to Orland and turn south onto Route 15, following the signs to the village, which is about 32 miles. Once in Stonington follow the road to the harbor at the bottom of the hill, turn left at the bank, and park across from the hardware store. Pay the proprietor for parking overnight. The mailboat leaves from the wharf below the hardware store.

Accommodations

Much of Isle au Haut's charm lies in its unspoiled and quiet nature, and access is limited. Acadia National Park provides three lean-to's at Duck Harbor, and reservations must be made months in advance, in writing. Tenting is not allowed, and there are no other accommodations; so if you arrive without a reservation you won't be allowed to stay the night unless there's a cancellation. The restrictions make the island a delightfully reclusive spot, though, and it is well worth the effort to plan ahead and obtain the necessary permits for an overnight stay. Applications must be postmarked April 1 or later and are available from:

Acadia National Park, RFD 1, Box 1, Bar Harbor, ME   04609.

When you arrive at Isle au Haut, stop at the information board at the head of the wharf and get a trail map, which is an essential item. (If there aren't any here, you can buy a good one at the village store — turn left onto the village road, and you'll see it shortly.) Remember that you'll have to hike about 5 miles to the campground, so plan accordingly, and pack lightly. If you're carrying a heavy pack and time is of the essence, the road is the fastest route. Drinking water and firewood are available at the campground.

One final note: please make every effort to respect the privacy of island residents.

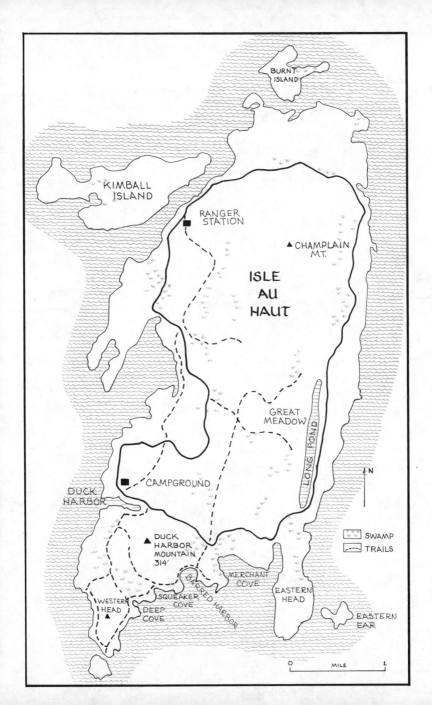

Chapter 14

Mount Desert Island

If any one place can be said to offer the best birding in eastern Maine — and some of the loveliest vistas along the entire Atlantic coast — it is Mount Desert Island. Of nearly 400 species of birds which have occured in Maine, at least 320 have been seen on Mount Desert. Some of these, such as Lesser Black-backed Gull, Chuck-will's-widow, Bewick's Wren, Lazuli Bunting, and LeConte's Spar-row, have provided first state records. Others — Swainson's Hawk,

Golden Eagle, Purple Gallinule, Royal Tern, Ash-throated Flycatcher, Lark Bunting, and Harris' Sparrow — have embellished an already noteworthy species list. At least 21 species of warblers nest on the island, and each year a great diversity of other birds is seen. Birding on Mount Desert is good year-round, and particularly from late May through at least September. The best time to see warblers is in the first two weeks in June, while late July and August are best for shorebirds and seabirds. Plan to spend at least a few days here. From Memorial Day through Labor Day the place is overrun with people, but despite the crowds you will find some fine birding.

Mount Desert lies 10 miles south of Ellsworth, connected to the mainland by bridge. About half the island lies within the boundaries of Acadia National Park, and scattered about the rest of the island are small communities and fishing villages. Roughly heart-shaped, the island measures 16 by 13 miles and is divided into east and west sides by Somes Sound, often described as the only true fjord in eastern North America. On the west side of the island is Blue Hill Bay and on the east side Frenchman Bay.

Named L'Isle de Monts Deserts in 1604 by Samuel de Champlain, Mount Desert is remarkable for its diversity of habitat. A string of 17 mountain peaks stretches across the island from southwest to northeast, and they range in elevation from 200 feet to 1530-foot Cadillac Mountain — the highest point on the Atlantic seaboard north of Rio de Janeiro. Geologists believe these granite-domed peaks may be only the remnants of a far larger mountain which was eroded by glaciers. These same glaciers left in their wake the numerous lakes and ponds that dot the island. Habitats on the island include dense spruce-fir forests and mixed deciduous woods, meadows and fields, heaths and bogs, freshwater and saltwater marshes, and a small (approximately 950 feet) sand beach. Botanically, the island is a contact zone for many northern and southern species, and this phenomenon is reflected in the avifauna. In general you will find birds with a northern affinity on the southwest side of Mount Desert and birds with a southern affinity on the northeast side of the island. The abundance of southern species on the island has increased notably since a forest fire in

1947 burned approximately 17,000 acres and opened up a large new habitat.

There are so many good birding spots on Mount Desert that the island really deserves a guide of its own. We touch upon only the highlights here, almost all of which lie within the park boundaries. (As you'll discover for yourself, you continually pass in and out of the park as you drive around the island. Please remember that private property *must* be respected.) If you have time to stop at only a few spots, the most productive are likely to be Ship Harbor, Wonderland, and Sieur de Monts Spring.

Stop at park headquarters to get a map of the island and a bird list. If you can, also get a copy of *Native Birds of Mount Desert Island and Acadia National Park* by James Bond (1971, The Academy of Natural Sciences of Philadelphia, 28 pp.). Though somewhat outdated, it still provides a wealth of information. If you plan to spend much time here, a U.S. Coast and Geodetic Survey (USGS) topographic map is helpful.

Precise directions are not included for every stop. You will find all these areas marked on the park map, and most are clearly marked on the park roads. For those which aren't, the appropriate directions are included.

Mount Desert Narrows

Check the Mount Desert Narrows at the causeway that connects the island and the mainland. In the winter, as long as there is open water, this is a good place to look for waterfowl and waterbirds, including an occasional Barrow's Goldeneye. Shorebirds are sometimes seen here on migration.

Bar Island Bar

The Bar Island Bar is a good place to see shorebirds and gulls in late summer and fall. Unfortunately it's also a good place to see lots of people, dogs, and motorbikes, but amazingly enough the birds rarely seem disturbed by this ruckus. Follow Route 3 into Bar Harbor and pass the CN Marine ferry terminal. At the Western Street Extension turn left, following signs for the business district.

In 0.3 miles turn left onto Bridge Street, and at low tide you'll see the bar directly ahead of you.

Bird the bar at low tide to mid-tide, when it's exposed. The cobble-like substrate attracts primarily Black-bellied Plovers, Ruddy Turnstones, and Semipalmated Sandpipers. Ruddy Turnstones are especially numerous, with a high count of 1,000 birds having been recorded in late August. This is also a reliable spot to see small numbers of Red Knots. Throughout the summer look for Bonaparte's and Laughing Gulls and Common Terns. Little Gull has been seen here in winter on rare occasion.

Sieur de Monts Spring

Sieur de Monts Spring is one of the best places on Mount Desert to see a wide variety of species, particularly during migration and also during the nesting season. Yellow-throated and Golden-winged Warblers are two of the most unusual birds that have been seen here. The predominantly deciduous woods here attract primarily birds of a southern affinity. Species you might see include American Woodcock, Black-billed Cuckoo, Great Crested Flycatcher, Eastern Pewee, Eastern Phoebe, Alder and Least Flycatchers, Wood Thrush, Veery, Red-Eyed Vireo, Black-and-White and Black-throated Green Warblers, American Redstart, Ovenbird, Scarlet Tanager, Rose-breasted Grosbeak, and Swamp Sparrow.

Bird the clearing around the spring in early morning, and then walk to Great Meadow, north of the spring. At the museum follow the carriage road away from the spring and through the birches. You'll soon cross another carriage trail, and in a half mile or so you'll intersect a much narrower trail, where the habitat becomes wetter and scrubbier. Go straight here, and the path will bring you out at the edge of Great Meadow. (The beavers that have a lodge along this trail sometimes flood the area and make it impassable.)

Also visit the Wild Gardens of Acadia at Sieur de Monts where 300 species of native plants are on display in 10 habitats which simulate the surrounding environment. Every species is labeled, so if you aren't as familiar as you'd like to be with Maine flora, this is a good place to bone up.

To reach Sieur de Monts, stay on Route 3 through Bar Harbor and follow signs for the spring.

Cadillac Mountain

Windswept Cadillac Mountain offers the most commanding view from Mount Desert Island. Rising abruptly above the sea and a host of smaller islands, it offers a spectacular vista that no one should pass up. You'll rarely see many birds of interest up here, except during hawk migration, when the mountain is an excellent vantage point. Visibility extends in all directions for several miles, and you can see a good deal of the surrounding coast from here. Follow the one-way Loop Road to the Cadillac Mountain road.

Otter Point

Otter Point overlooks Frenchman Bay from the southeastern tip of Mount Desert and is covered by a stand of spruce-fir forest, much of which has been blown down. The path that leads through the woods is an excellent place to look for migrant and nesting warblers. A few spruce woods specialties you might see at any time of year include Black-backed Three-toed Woodpecker (Northern Three-toed Woodpecker also has been seen here), Boreal Chickadee, and Gray Jay. Otter Point is reached from the one-way Loop Road. The trail starts at the north end of the parking lot.

Seawall Bog

Seawall Bog, or the Big Heath, is a large sphagnum bog on the north side of Route 102A. It is a lovely area, vegetated with Sheep Laurel, Leatherleaf, Black Spruce, sundews, Pitcher Plant, and exquisite bog orchids, including *Arethusa* and *Calapogon*. The highlights of the area ornithologically are nesting Yellow-bellied Flycatchers, Palm Warblers, and Lincoln's Sparrows. Come in early June, as the Palm Warblers are early nesters and may be feeding young by the middle of the month. Along the edges of the bog look for Boreal Chickadees, Ruby-crowned Kinglets, and other spruce woods songbirds.

Enter the bog across from the Wonderland parking lot, looking carefully for several small trails that lead into it. *Please:* bird the bog from the edge, and stay on the well-trodden paths. *The plant life is very fragile.*

Wonderland

Wonderland, despite its Disney-like name, is another fine birding spot. Though just across the road from the Big Heath, it offers an entirely different habitat. A wide trail leads 0.6 miles through mixed deciduous and coniferous woods, across a dry and open area of lichen-covered ledges and Pitch Pine, and then enters a tall grove of spruces along the shore. Like Ship Harbor just beyond it, Wonderland is a particularly good place to see migrant and nesting warblers, including Blackpolls some years. The parking lot and trail are on the south side of Route 102A.

Ship Harbor

Ship Harbor is one of the loveliest spots on Mount Desert and one of the best birding areas. At least 18 species of warblers and many of the unusual northern landbirds nest here. At the head of the harbor is a sunny and open clearing and beyond it a trail that leads 1.6 miles through the woods to the shore and back. In 1936 a pair of Cape May Warblers that nested here were a first nesting record for the United States.

Look for nesting and migrant warblers at Ship Harbor and for northern specialties such as Black-backed Three-toed Woodpecker, Yellow-bellied, Alder, Least, and Olive-sided Flycatchers, Gray Jay, Boreal Chickadee, Swainson's Thrush, Ruby and Golden-crowned Kinglets, and Red and White-winged Crossbills. A Bewick's Wren seen here in 1971 provided a first and thus far only state record.

The Ship Harbor parking lot is on the south side of Route 102A.

Bass Harbor Head and Marsh

Bass Harbor Head offers an extensive stand of spruce-fir woods and is another good spot to see migrant and nesting warblers (particularly Bay-breasted) and spruce woods specialties. Follow signs

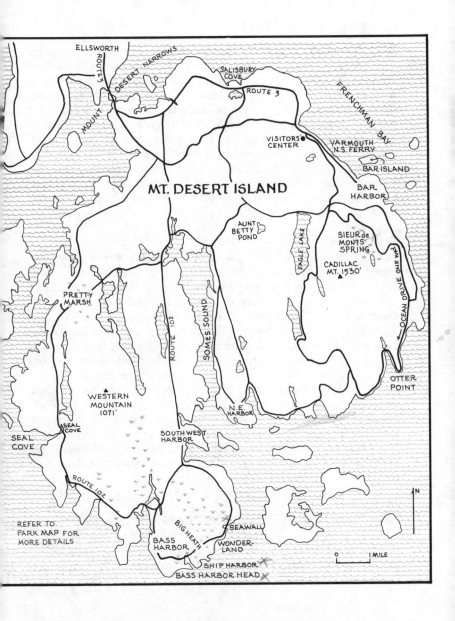

from Route 102A to Bass Harbor Head, where you can park. Species seen on occasion include Black-backed Three-toed Woodpecker, Gray Jay, and Boreal Chickadee. It's also a good spot to scan for waterfowl and seabirds. King Eider and Harlequin Duck are occasionally seen in winter. Harbor Porpoises are often reported here in summer. Scan from the lighthouse at any time of year, and during migration and in summer walk the half mile of road back to Route 102A to look for warblers and other landbirds.

Bass Harbor Marsh, north of the lighthouse and also on Route 102A, is a good place to see wading birds and nesting Sharp-tailed Sparrows in spring and summer. You can scan it from the roadside.

Boat Trips
Acadia National Park and private individuals offer a variety of boat trips from Mount Desert throughout the summer, and information on them is available from park headquarters. Any of the trips provides a good opportunity to see offshore island nesters: Double-crested Cormorants, Great Blue Herons, Common Eiders, Bald Eagles, Osprey, Greater Black-backed and Herring Gulls, Common and Arctic Terns, and Black Guillemots. A trip to Mount Desert Rock, about 23 miles offshore, can be particularly productive as it offers a chance to see more pelagic species than do the harbor trips. From mid-June through September you have a good chance of seeing Northern Fulmar, Greater, Sooty, and possibly Manx and Cory's Shearwaters, Wilson's Storm Petrel, Northern Gannet, Northern and Red Phalaropes (primarily late summer and fall, with the former far more abundant), Black-legged Kittiwake, and possibly a Parasitic Jaeger, Great Skua, or Atlantic Puffin.

Directions
Mount Desert Island is reached from Route 3 in Ellsworth.

Accommodations
Motels and campgrounds, including two within the park, are numerous but crowded in summer.

Chapter 15

M.V. *Bluenose*

One of the greatest delights of birding on the Maine coast is a chance to bird the *Bluenose*, the 346-foot Canadian National ferry that plies the 200-mile round-trip between Bar Harbor and Yarmouth, Nova Scotia. This is one of the most famous pelagic trips on the east coast, and although increasing numbers of whale and seabird trips are being offered every year, it still provides the only regular opportunity for true pelagic birding in Maine. Davis Finch, Will Russell, and Edward Thompson, authors of *Pelagic Birds in the Gulf of Maine*, call the *Bluenose* "ornithologically the most studied oceanic route in the East." The ferry operates from the end of May through October, crossing daily from mid-June through September and 3 times weekly the remainder of the season. The best time to make the trip is from mid-June through August, when shearwaters and petrels are most abundant. As fall pushes on and the cold begins to bite in earnest, "tubenoses" dwindle but the chance of seeing unusual gulls and alcids, particularly Thick-billed Murres and Dovekies, increases.

Traveling almost due east from Bar Harbor to Yarmouth, the *Bluenose* crosses the northern edge of the Gulf of Maine and the mouth of the Bay of Fundy. Over much of this course vertical circulation brings to the surface nutrient-rich bottom waters that make this area renowned for its fisheries and seabird populations. Two areas along the course — the edge of the Grand Manan Bank about 10 miles off the Maine coast and Lurcher Shoal along the southwest shore of Nova Scotia — are particularly productive, and it is here that you often see the greatest concentrations of birds.

The best place to position yourself on the *Bluenose* is on the open bow where you have the greatest visibility. From mid-June through September the most commonly seen species are Northern Fulmar, Greater, Sooty, and Manx Shearwaters (these last 3 in order of decreasing likelihood), Leach's and Wilson's Storm Petrels (the latter far more abundant), Northern Gannet, Common Eider, Northern and Red Phalaropes (primarily late summer and early fall, with Northerns passing through earlier than Reds), Parasitic Jaeger, Great Skua, Greater Black-backed and Herring Gulls (year-round), Common and Arctic Terns (the former primarily in French-man Bay), Black Guillemot (also primarily in Frenchman Bay), and Atlantic Puffin. Aside from Greater Black-backed and Herring Gulls, the most abundant species typically are Wilson's Storm Petrel and Greater Shearwater. In recent summers Cory's Shear-water has been seen regularly in small numbers, but this may be a temporary phenomenon caused perhaps by unusually warm waters. Species less likely to be encountered in the summer but nonetheless occasional are Pomarine Jaeger, Razorbill, Thin-billed Murre, Ring-billed, Laughing, and Bonaparte's Gulls (all primarily in Frenchman Bay and the last after mid-July), and Black-legged Kittiwake. Sailing out of Bar Harbor look for nesting Ospreys and possibly Bald Eagles. In the fall you may see a good variety of waterfowl, and at any time of year it is worth scanning the flocks of Common Eiders for a King Eider.

Unfortunately the *Bluenose* no longer operates from November through May, and the last crossing you can make is in late October. You can expect to see good numbers of Northern Fulmars, Northern Gannets, Bonaparte's Gulls, and Black-legged Kittiwakes then, smaller numbers of Greater Shearwaters, and possibly Leach's Storm Petrels, Red Phalaropes, and Pomarine or Parasitic Jaegers. Although it's on the early side, look also for Glaucous and Iceland Gulls and for alcids, particularly Thick-billed Murres and Dovekies. In Yarmouth Harbor look for Black-headed Gulls, which sometimes are seen there from fall through spring.

Exceptionally rare sightings from the *Bluenose* in recent years include Yellow-nosed Albatross, Little Shearwater, Long-tailed Jaeger, Sabine's Gull, and Royal Tern — all of which occurred in summer or early fall. In summer the *Bluenose* also provides an excellent opportunity for whale watching.

A prerequisite for anyone planning to do the *Bluenose* is *Pelagic Birds in the Gulf of Maine* by Davis W. Finch, William C. Russell, and Edward V. Thompson. Based on observations from the *Bluenose*, it provides a wealth of information on distribution and abundance as well as extensive notes on identification. You can find it in *American Birds*, Vol. 32, No. 2, 1978, pp. 140-155 and Vol. 32, No. 3, 1978, pp. 281-294, or order a reprint from:

American Birds
950 Third Avenue
New York, N.Y. 10002

Directions
From mid-June through September the *Bluenose* crosses daily, leaving Bar Harbor at 8:00 A.M. Eastern Daylight Time (EDT) and departing Yarmouth at 4:30 P.M. Atlantic Daylight Time (ADT, one hour ahead of EDT). The trip takes about 6 hours each way, with a 90-minute layover in Yarmouth. From the end of May through mid-June and in October the ferry crosses three times weekly, leaving Bar Harbor 8:00 A.M. EDT on Tuesdays, Thursdays, and Saturdays and departing Yarmouth at 9:00 A.M. ADT on Mondays, Wednesdays, and Fridays. In October check the schedule for reversion to standard time.

Advance reservations are suggested. For further information write or call:

CN Marine Reservations Bureau
P.O. Box 250
North Sydney, Nova Scotia
B2A 3M3 CANADA

Toll-free numbers:
(Maine) 1-800-432-7344
(northeastern U.S.) 1-800-341-7981

The Canadian National ferry terminal in Bar Harbor is conspicuously located on Route 3 on the north side of town.

Accommodations
Motels are plentiful in Bar Harbor and Yarmouth, and camping is available on both sides as well.

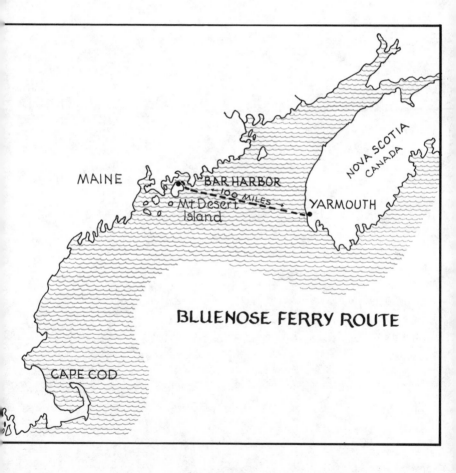

Chapter 16

Schoodic Point

Situated across Frenchman Bay and due east of Mount Desert Island lies another outpost of Acadia National Park — Schoodic Point. Comprising roughly 2,000 acres on the tip of Schoodic Peninsula, it is the only part of Acadia located on the mainland. Even on a coast legendary for its beauty, Schoodic Point is an exceptionally lovely spot, whether shrouded in fog or sparkling in the sunlight. It is also a fine birding area, well worth a visit at any time of year. As on the southwest portion of Mount Desert, the dense, though less extensive, spruce-fir woods here are especially good for nesting warblers and for boreal specialties year-round. Schoodic Point also is a fine place to see seabirds, waterfowl, and migrating passerines. Plan to spend a half day or more here at any time of year.

Schoodic Point is accessible year-round from a two-lane, one-way loop road that runs along the shore. When you cross the park boundary scan Mosquito Harbor and then immediately afterwards, on your right, Frazier Point for seabirds and waterfowl. In winter check the Common Goldeneyes that gather here for an occasional Barrow's Goldeneye.

Continue south from Frazier Point and in 2.3 miles you'll see a gravel road on the left which leads 1 mile up to Schoodic Head. Drive or hike to the top and then hike the 0.2 miles to the 440-foot summit. A 1-mile trail descends from Schoodic Head to the Anvil, a smaller peak south of Schoodic Head, and ends on the loop road 0.3 miles south of the gravel road. Although you can do some good birding from the roadside (at least when the traffic isn't too heavy), hiking the gravel road and the Schoodic Head trails greatly increases your chance of finding spruce-fir specialties. Look year-round for Spruce Grouse, Black-backed Three-toed Woodpecker (Northern Three-toed Woodpecker also has been seen here on rare occasion), Gray Jay, Northern Raven, and Boreal Chickadee. Throughout the nesting season look for Olive-sided, Yellow-bellied, and Least Flycatchers, Winter Wren, Swainson's Thrush, Ruby-crowned Kinglet, and several warblers, including Tennessee, Magnolia, Cape May, Black-throated Blue, Bay-breasted, and Blackpoll. In winter look for the usual northern finches, most of which are erratic in their occurrence. Red and White-winged Crossbills can be seen at any time of year.

Just beyond the base of the gravel road is a marshy pond worth checking on the left and 0.5 miles beyond that a salt marsh on the left. Look here especially for nesting Sharp-tailed Sparrows.

Schoodic Point lies 1.4 miles beyond the gravel road (fork right at the triangle) and offers an excellent vantage point over open ocean. In the summer look here for Common Eiders (often with ducklings), Osprey, Laughing and Bonaparte's Gulls, Common and Arctic Terns, and Black Guillemots. In winter look for common seabirds and waterfowl and for such hard-to-find species as Harlequin Duck, King Eider, Glaucous and Iceland Gulls, Black-legged Kittiwake, and all 6 alcids. Brant are occasionally seen in March and April, and at any time of year (except the dead of winter) scan carefully for a Northern Gannet. During migration as many as

100-plus birds have been seen here in a single day. Look also for a Bald Eagle at any time of year, particularly in winter.

Species of particular note seen at Schoodic Point include a breeding-plumage Arctic Loon which provided a second state record in June 1978; an Eared Grebe in March 1977 which was a fifth state record; and a Black-headed Gull.

Directions

To reach Schoodic Point turn south off Route 1 onto Route 186 in West Gouldsboro and continue 6.8 miles to Winter Harbor. Turn left at the waterfront and in 0.6 miles right, following signs for Acadia National Park. This is the beginning of the loop road. (If you turn south off Route 1 onto Route 186 in Gouldsboro, continue past Prospect Harbor; you'll see the sign for Acadia National Park before you reach Winter Harbor.) The loop road brings you back out on Route 186 east of Winter Harbor.

Accommodations

The nearest motels are in Ellsworth and Milbridge. The nearest campgrounds are in Ellsworth and Steuben. There is no camping at Schoodic Point.

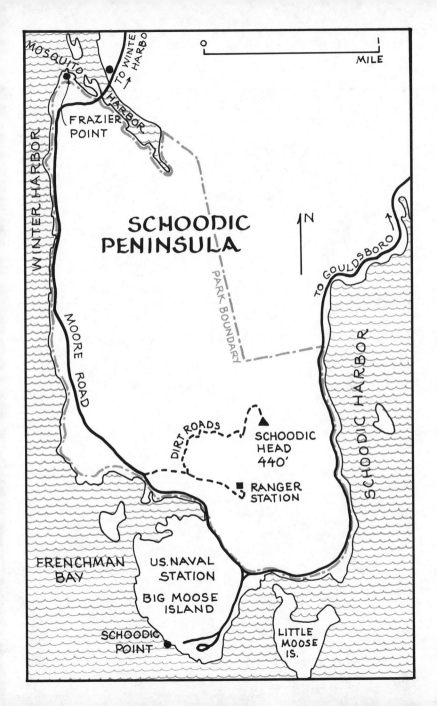

Washington County

Chapter 17

Deblois Barrens and Addison Marsh

Deblois Barrens

The blueberry barrens of Washington County are a unique habitat in Maine, and the most extensive of these are the Deblois Barrens north of Cherryfield. In a state where some 90 percent of the land is forested, here you find thousands of acres of open, tundralike fields once scoured by glaciers and now distinguished by rocky debris, scattered bogs, and numerous ridges, kettleholes, and outwash plains. Late Lowbush Blueberry is the dominant vegetation, interspersed with Red Pine and alder thickets. Although the birding is not diverse on blueberry barrens, they are good places, particularly during the breeding season, to look for certain species you may not see elsewhere. Nesting Upland Sandpipers are the highlight of the Deblois Barrens. Although the barrens are privately owned, you can scan them from Route 193 which runs from Cherryfield north to Route 9. The best time to visit this area is in June, as the blueberries get sprayed with pesticides through the rest of the summer.

During the nesting season species which you should look for on and around the barrens include Northern Harrier, Upland Sandpipers (in 1980 at least 50 pairs nested in 12 loose colonies from Deblois to Columbia), Black-billed and sometimes Yellow-billed Cuckoos (especially in years of heavy tent caterpillar infestations), Whip-poor-wills, Yellow-bellied, Alder, and Least Flycatchers, Palm and Mourning Warblers, Bobolinks, Indigo Buntings, and Vesper Sparrows, the last often being abundant. Mixed flocks of Horned Larks and Snow Buntings sometimes are abundant during migration, and although it's a bit far from the coast, you might see Whimbrels in the fall. In winter this can be — with luck — a good place to see hawks, owls, and Northern Shrikes.

Directions

To reach the Deblois Barrens take Route 193 north from Route 1 in Cherryfield. You'll soon see the barrens on either side of the road, and they continue about 12 miles. For another route into the barrens, go only 1.4 miles north on Route 193 and fork right onto Ridge Road.

As you'll soon discover for yourself, there are hundreds of obscure dirt roads through the barrens. Presumably they are all private property, but many people wander at will along them. Be advised that it's easy to get lost anytime you get off Route 193.

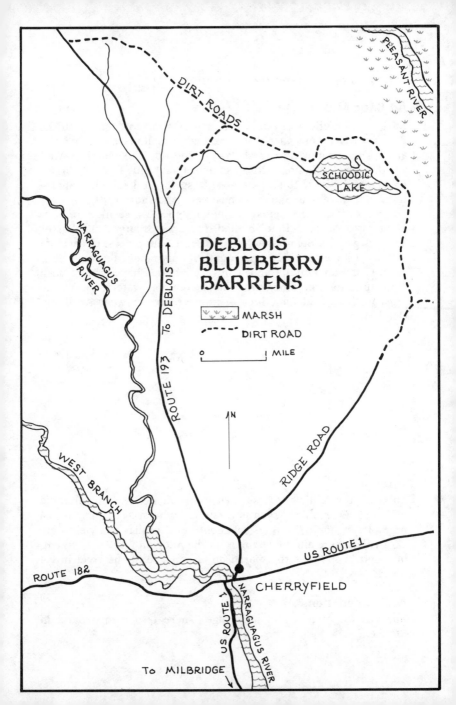

DEBLOIS
BLUEBERRY
BARRENS

MARSH
DIRT ROAD
0 — — 1 MILE

PLEASANT RIVER

SCHOODIC LAKE

DIRT ROADS

NARRAGUAGUS RIVER

TO DEBLOIS

ROUTE 193

WEST BRANCH

RIDGE ROAD

N

ROUTE 182

CHERRYFIELD

US ROUTE 1

US ROUTE 1

NARRAGUAGUS RIVER

To MILBRIDGE

Addison Marsh

East of Cherryfield in Addison is a good-sized salt marsh on the Pleasant River. On a part of the coast where salt marshes generally are small and few and far between, the Addison marsh is well worth a check. Wading birds, primarily Great Blue Herons, Snowy Egrets, and Glossy Ibises, are seen in spring and summer; Sharp-tailed and Savannah Sparrows nest here, and shorebirds stop over on migration. The most common species seen here are Semipalmated and Black-bellied Plovers, Greater and Lesser Yellowlegs, and Semipalmated and Least Sandpipers. Occasional Willets and Western, Pectoral, and Stilt Sandpipers also have been seen. Common Pintails and a few Northern Shovelers are seen from time to time along with more common waterfowl. You're most likely to find something of interest here between April and October.

Directions

To reach the Addison marsh turn south off Route 1 in Columbia Falls (not Columbia, which is a few miles west). Fork left in 0.4 miles, left again in 0.1 miles, and continue 2.1 miles to a yield sign. Go straight here and in 0.4 miles, at the Addison Fire Department, bear left. You'll see the marsh on either side of the road in 0.4 miles.

Accommodations

The nearest motel is in Milbridge. There is a campground in Steuben.

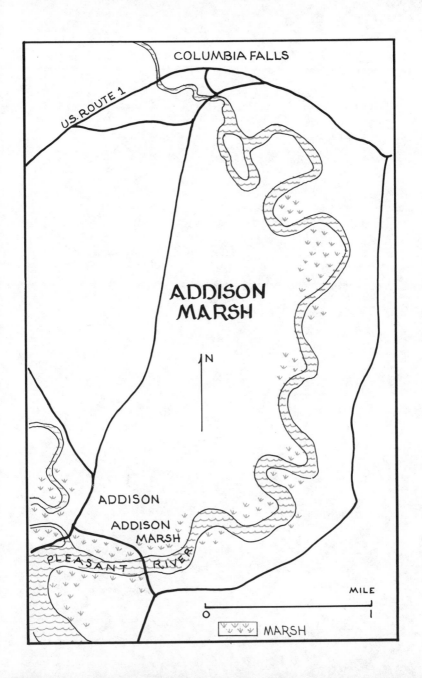

COLUMBIA FALLS

U.S. ROUTE 1

ADDISON
MARSH

N

ADDISON

ADDISON
MARSH

PLEASANT RIVER

MILE

0   1

MARSH

Chapter 18

Machias Seal Island and Machias Bay Region

Anyone interested in seabirds will want to make a trip to Machias Seal Island, for even along a coast which is famous for its enchanting seabird islands, Machias Seal is something special. Serving as a Canadian lighthouse outpost since 1832, the island lies in the Bay of Fundy 10 miles south of Cutler and boasts nesting colonies of Common and Arctic Terns, Atlantic Puffins, Razorbills, and Leach's Storm Petrels. Fortunately it is the most accessible as well as one of the most delightful of the Gulf of Maine's many seabird islands. The best time to visit is between mid-June and early July when nesting activity is at its peak.

While a trip to Machias Seal is a highlight along this part of the coast, the mainland around Machias Bay also offers productive birding. Route 191 from East Machias east to Cutler and West Lubec is one of the best areas on the coast to look for wintering hawks and owls and for boreal species (many of which nest here) year-round. It also offers some good shorebirding during spring and fall migration. At any time of year you can spend the better part of a day exploring this area.

Machias Seal Island

Machias Seal is a 15-acre treeless island vegetated primarily by asters, wild parsleys, docks, grasses, sedges, and herbs. The lighthouse and three keepers' houses stand on the highest ground, and boardwalks and paths lead out to the nesting colonies. The terns nest over a large portion of the island on high grassy areas, while the puffins and Razorbills nest among the rocks and ledges on the southwest shore. Two blinds enable you to watch and photograph the birds from just a few feet away.

According to recent surveys by the Canadian Wildlife Service, Machias Seal supports an estimated 1,500 pairs of Arctic Terns, 100 pairs of Common Terns, 800 pairs of Atlantic Puffins, and 40 pairs of Razorbills. While the alcid populations appear to be stable, the tern populations apparently are declining. Since 1979 1 pair of Roseate Terns has nested on the island. The terns' nesting activities are well under way by early June, so that by mid-July most young birds are on the wing. The puffins' and Razorbills' nesting activities peak about mid-June when most of the young hatch, and by mid-August many of the birds have left.

A few hundred pairs of Leach's Storm Petrels and small numbers of Spotted Sandpipers, Tree and Barn Swallows, and Savannah Sparrows also nest on Machias Seal. The petrels nest in underground burrows on the northeast side of the island and are rarely seen since they come and go from their nesting colonies only after dark. Thin-billed Murres don't nest on the island, but oftentimes you can see a few sitting on the rocks among the puffins and the Razorbills or sitting on the water offshore.

In late summer keep your eyes open for migrants or storm-tossed vagrants on the island — over a hundred species, including some that are rare or unusual, have been recorded here.

En route to and from Machias Seal from mid-June through August look for Northern Fulmars, Greater, Sooty, and Manx Shearwaters, Wilson's Storm Petrels, Northern Gannets, Northern and Red Phalaropes (late summer), Parasitic Jaegers, and Black-legged Kittiwakes. In Cutler harbor look for Bald Eagles.

You might want to ask your boatman to take you around North Rock where you sometimes can see Gray Seals, or "Horseheads."

In recent years Machias Seal has become a mecca for naturalists and photographers, and the growing number of people has prompted concern for the birds' welfare. Unfortunately enthusiastic visitors can wreak havoc, albeit unwittingly, on a seabird nesting island. Please — enjoy the considerable freedom you're allowed on this delightful island and observe the few guidelines.

To arrange a trip to Machias Seal Island write or call:

Capt. Barna Norton
Jonesport, ME 04640
(207) 497-5933

Barna makes a trip out of Cutler (or sometimes Jonesport) almost every day throughout the summer, leaving at 7 A.M. and returning by noon or so. The trip out takes about an hour, and depending on weather and tide conditions you have anywhere from one to three hours on the island. Landing is possible only on a calm day. In the event that you can't land, the trip still provides a fine opportunity to see the birds at close range. You should make reservations with Barna as early as you can.

Pack whatever food and drink you'll need, a hat to protect you from the onslaught of the terns, raingear, and something to protect cameras and binoculars from spray on the boat.

Machias Bay Region

The 28 miles along Route 191 from East Machias to West Lubec offer the best birding in the Machias Bay area. There is no public property along the way, but you can do some fine birding from the roadside. Habitats you'll encounter include river and bay, alder swales, blueberry barrens, open fields, spruce-fir and mixed deciduous woods, mud flats and gravel bars, and heaths. At any time of year you're likely to see something of interest here. The following stops, which can be worked in a loop, are areas especially worth checking.

Starting on Route 1 in Machias, stop first at the Machias and East Machias rivers where Route 1 crosses them. These are good places to see waterfowl, including an occasional Barrow's Goldeneye in winter, and at any time of year a Bald Eagle.

In East Machias turn south onto Route 191 and continue 6.8 miles to the bridge at Holmes Creek where you can pull over and scan. The flats to your right here are good for shorebirds on spring and fall migration. Short-billed Dowitchers are especially numerous, with as many as 700 having been reported here at once, and good numbers of Black-bellied Plovers and Greater and Lesser Yellowlegs also stop over. Red Knots and pectoral Sandpipers are occasional, while Hudsonian and Marbled Godwit, Willet, Long-billed Dowitcher, and Western Sandpiper are rare. In the salt marsh that borders the creek look and listen for nesting Sharp-tailed Sparrows.

About 1 mile south of Holmes Creek an extensive stand of spruce-fir woods begins on either side of the road and continues nearly 3 miles. Boreal nesters which you should look for (some year-round) here include Spruce Grouse, Black-backed Three-toed Woodpecker, Gray Jay, Northern Raven, Boreal Chickadee, Swainson's Thrush, Ruby-crowned Kinglet, and several species of warblers, including Tennessee, Cape May, and Bay-breasted. One place especially worth checking is 2.2 miles south of Holmes Creek on the left where you see a conspicuous stand of dead and blown down conifers — a known nesting spot for Black-backed Three-toed Woodpeckers. Look for bare patches on the trees where the birds have chipped off thin layers of bark.

Continue south on Route 191 and 0.6 miles after the road turns sharply to the left stop at Turner's Bridge on Little Machias Bay. The extensive flats here are another spot worth checking for migrant shorebirds. This is a particularly reliable place to see good numbers of Whimbrels on fall migration.

Cutler harbor, 2.5 miles south of Turner's Bridge, is worth

checking year-round for waterfowl, seabirds, and an occasional Bald Eagle.

In Cutler Route 191 turns north and continues about 15 miles to West Lubec, and along most of the way you'll see extensive blueberry barrens interspersed with open fields and alder swales. In the summer this stretch of road can be a good place to look for nesting Northern Harriers and Vesper Sparrows and during migration for Whimbrels (fall) and hawks, particularly accipiters and falcons. From November through March this is one of the best places on the coast to look for raptors, occurring some years in unusually high numbers. It tends to be a hit or miss area, but species you should look for here include Goshawk, Sharp-shinned, Red-tailed, and Rough-legged Hawks, occasionally Northern Harriers, Great Horned, Snowy, Hawk, Barred, and Short-eared Owls, and Northern Shrike. Horned Larks and Snow Buntings sometimes are abundant, especially on migration, and it's worth scanning them for Lapland Longspurs. Look too for Common Redpolls and other wintering finches. Red Foxes and Coyotes can also be seen here.

In summer look around boggy areas on Route 191 for nesting Palm Warblers and Lincoln's Sparrows and around alder swales for Alder Flycatchers and Wilson's Warblers. Interestingly, Willow Flycatchers were reported to be nesting in this area in 1979 in East Machias.

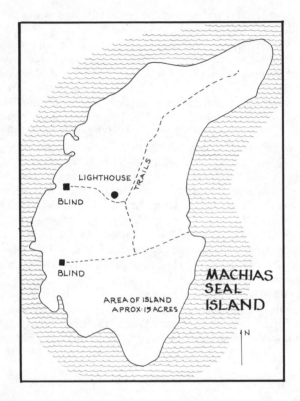

Directions
Route 191 turns south off Route 1 in East Machias and joins Route 189 in West Lubec. Whichever way you're traveling, allow some time to stop at Helen's Restaurant in Machias, which is famous with birders and nonbirders alike for its superb pies.

Accommodations
There are a few motels open year-round in Machias and Lubec. The closest campgrounds are in Jonesboro and on Campobello Island, New Brunswick.

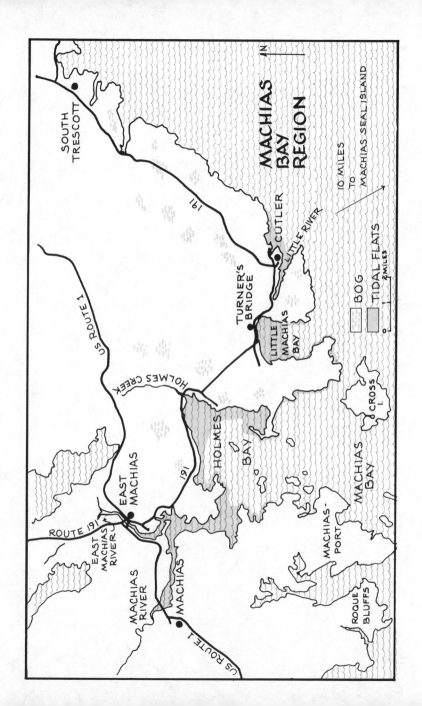

MACHIAS BAY REGION

SOUTH TRESCOTT

US ROUTE 1

CUTLER

LITTLE RIVER

191

TURNER'S BRIDGE

LITTLE MACHIAS BAY

HOLMES CREEK

HOLMES BAY

CROSS I.

EAST MACHIAS

EAST MACHIAS RIVER

ROUTE 191

191

MACHIAS-PORT

MACHIAS BAY

MACHIAS RIVER

MACHIAS

US ROUTE 1

ROQUE BLUFFS

N

10 MILES TO MACHIAS SEAL ISLAND

BOG

TIDAL FLATS

0   1   2 MILES

Chapter 19

Lubec

Lubec Flats
Quoddy Head Light
Campobello Island, New Brunswick

Relatively few people visit the small town of Lubec on lower Passamaquoddy Bay, but of those who do it's a safe bet that more than a few are birdwatchers. Lubec is well known primarily as a shorebirding area, and together with the Eastport flats to the north across Cobscook Bay this area offers some of the finest shorebirding in Maine. Nearby Quoddy Head Light at the end of the neck is an excellent vantage point from which to scan for seabirds and ducks, particularly in winter, and the extensive spruce-fir forest there is a good place to look for nesting warblers and for boreal specialties. Spruce Grouse, Gray Jay, and Boreal Chickadee are permanent residents. Campobello Island, New Brunswick, connected to Lubec by bridge, also offers some fine birding and is a particularly good spot to see phalaropes, gulls, and alcids. Lubec is well worth a visit at any time of year. At the height of the season, in late summer and fall, plan to spend at least a full day.

Lubec Flats

Lubec's most outstanding feature is the Lubec flats on West Quoddy Head, a narrow arm of land that extends 2 miles east into the Grand Manan Channel and is the easternmost point of land in the United States. A land of extremes, West Quoddy Head is bordered on the north by extensive mudflats, to the south and east by bold rocky headlands, and is washed by 13- to 26- foot tides. Much of the neck lies within the boundaries of Quoddy Head State Park. The Lubec flats lie along the northwestern shore of the peninsula and attract some of the largest concentrations of shorebirds to be found anywhere in Maine. As elsewhere, the fall migration is far more pronounced than the spring, and it generally peaks here in mid-August. The area is well worth a visit anytime from mid-July well into the fall.

The best way to work the Lubec flats is to park along the roadside 0.6 miles down the Quoddy Head road (you'll see a small parking space here on the left), scramble down the bank to the shore, and work your way east up the flats. The shore will curve around to your left and you'll see a long narrow spit (covered at high tide) and just beyond it a prominent rise, which usually is the best place from which to scan. Bird the area on a mid-tide, two to three hours before or after high tide. At high tide this area is nearly impossible to work, unless you like wading up to your knees in frigid water, and at low tide the birds are too widely dispersed to be studied closely. As elsewhere, make every effort not to disturb birds here, especially where such large numbers gather.

Shorebirds regularly seen at Lubec include Semipalmated and Black-bellied Plovers, Ruddy Turnstones, Greater and Lesser Yellowlegs, Red Knots, White-rumped and Least Sandpipers, Dunlin, Semipalmated Sandpipers, and Sanderling. The area is especially good for Semipalmated and Least Sandpipers, and counts of 10,000 to 15,000 birds are not uncommon from late July through August, with Semipalmateds far more abundant than Leasts. Black-bellied Plovers appear in large numbers in early August and peak in late August and September, with high counts of up to 2,000 birds. Look for smaller though regular flocks of Semipalmated Plovers (high counts of up to 400), White-rumped

Sandpipers (300), and Ruddy Turnstones (150), with Sanderlings (400) and Dunlin following later in the season. Both Greater and Lesser Yellowlegs are regular though rarely numerous, as is true of Red Knots (high count of 100 birds).

Less common species at Lubec are Killdeer, Lesser Golden Plover, Whimbrel, Willet, Solitary and Spotted Sandpipers, Short-billed Dowitcher, and Western Sandpiper. American Avocet, Baird's Sandpiper, Stilt Sandpiper, and Marbled Godwit are rare, but a few may be seen from year to year. In short, keep your eyes open and examine birds carefully, as sheer numbers make anything a possibility here. This is one of two places in Maine where Curlew Sandpiper has been seen. The species composition of spring migration is similar to that of fall, though no large number of any species passes through.

At high tide, when the Lubec flats are flooded, hundreds and sometimes thousands of gulls roost on the water, and at any time of year they merit careful scanning. Look for small gulls year-round, particularly in late summer and fall, and in winter for Glaucous, Iceland, and possibly Black-headed Gulls. In March and April this is a reliable spot to see large numbers of Brant (high counts of 1,500 to 2,000), sometimes lingering into May.

In addition to checking the flats, check the raised bog on your right 0.3 miles down the Quoddy Head road. This is Carrying Place Bog, a fascinating area in its own right, which supports several plant species, including Cloudberry and Reindeer Moss, typical of more northern areas. You should not walk into the bog, as the plant life is fragile, but you can scan it easily from the roadside. This is a good place to look for nesting Palm Warblers and Lincoln's Sparrows, and occasionally a few shorebirds roost along the stream here at high tide. In the winter look carefully for a hawk, owl, or Northern Shrike.

Quoddy Head Light
Quoddy Head Light at the end of West Quoddy Head offers an excellent vantage point over open ocean and an extensive stand of spruce-fir forest. Scan from the light itself, and then walk the long

path from the south end of the parking lot through the woods and along the rocky shore. In the summer Quoddy Head Light is a good place to look for a variety of seabirds and for boreal nesters: Spruce Grouse, Black-backed Three-toed Woodpecker, Gray Jay, Northern Raven, Boreal Chickadee (these 5 species year-round), Swainson's Thrush, Ruby-crowned Kinglet, and Magnolia, Cape May, Black-throated Blue, Bay-breasted, and Blackpoll Warblers all are possibilities here. This is also a good place to see whales in summer.

In winter look offshore for Harlequin Ducks and an occasional King Eider, good numbers of Black-legged Kittiwakes, and alcids. Black Guillemots are regular throughout the winter, and Razorbills, Thin-billed and Thick-billed Murres, and Dovekies are occasional. Look also for Purple Sandpipers. At any time of year except the dead of winter this is a good place to scan for a Northern Gannet.

Campobello Island, New Brunswick

Campobello Island, New Brunswick is connected to Lubec by bridge and measures about 9 by 3 miles. A lovely island well known as the former summer home of Franklin and Eleanor Roosevelt, it is also a fine birding spot. Campobello is a particularly good spot to see phalaropes and unusual gulls in late summer and early fall, and in winter it's a good place to look for alcids and other seabirds. Look also for migrant hawks and landbirds. The following areas, which can be worked in a loop, are especially worth checking.

From Canadian customs on the south end of Campobello go 2.2 miles north where you'll see Friar Bay on the left. This is worth scanning year-round for gulls and for ducks and alcids in winter.

From Friar Bay continue another 0.3 miles north, fork left at the big T-intersection, and in 0.7 miles you'll see a small road on the left with a sign for the Deer Island ferry. From mid-August to Labor day, when the ferry stops running, it provides an outstanding opportunity to see a phenomenal concentration of Northern Phalaropes and gulls. (See Deer Island Ferry, Eastport, next chapter).

Return to the T-intersection and continue straight or, if

you're coming from Friar Bay, turn right here. In 2.3 miles you'll see a dump on your right, and this is worth checking at any time of year for gulls and Northern Ravens.

Continue north past the dump and in 3.2 miles stop at Wilson's Beach. Overlooking the lower end of Head Harbor Passage, this is a particularly good spot to see Northern Phalaropes in late summer and fall and is a good place to see seabirds throughout the winter.

Head Harbor Light is 2.3 miles north of Wilson's Beach and offers a fine vantage point over open ocean. This is a particularly reliable spot to see Black-legged Kittiwakes and alcids in winter. At low tide you can cross the gravel bar to the lighthouse. Like Quoddy Head in Lubec, this is a good spot to see whales in summer.

Turning around at Head Harbor, drive 7.5 miles south and turn left toward Herring Cove. In 1.1 miles you'll see a long, crescent-shaped gravel beach here. Park and walk the beach, which can be a good place to scan for seabirds year-round.

Back on the main road continue 0.5 miles south to the T-intersection, turn left, and in 1 mile turn left again onto Glensevern Road toward Raccoon Point. This brings you out at the southern end of Herring Cove. If the road is open, continue on to Liberty Point on the southeast end of the island where there are several marshes and bogs worth investigating in the summer and during migration.

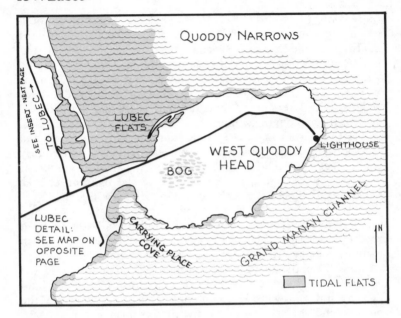

Directions

To reach Lubec take Route 189 North from Route 1 in Whiting. Continue 10.1 miles and turn right, and in 2.8 miles turn left onto the Quoddy Head Road. In 0.3 miles you'll see Carrying Place Bog on your right and in another 0.3 miles the easiest access to the Lubec flats. From here Quoddy Head Light is another 1.3 miles. To reach Campobello go back to Route 189 and turn right, and in 0.8 miles fork right at the blinking light. You'll see the Lubec-Campobello bridge in 1.3 miles. As long as you're a U.S. citizen you can cross the border easily without a passport. Get a map of Campobello at the Friar Bay Motor Lodge.

Accommodations

There are a few motels, which are open only during the tourist season, in Lubec and on Campobello. The nearest campgrounds are on Campobello and at Cobscook Bay State Park north of Whiting.

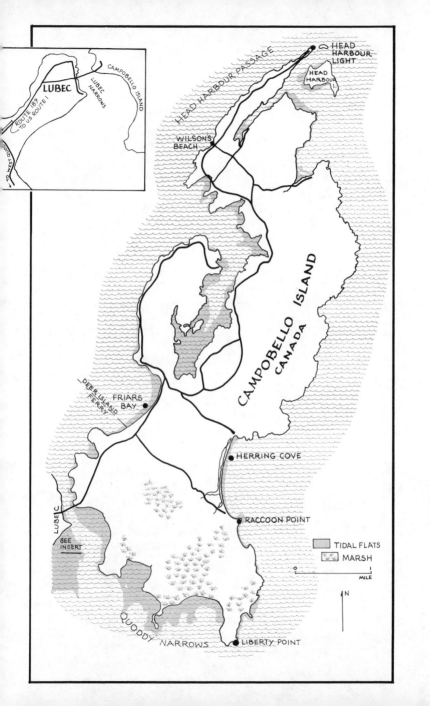

LUBEC

CAMPOBELLO ISLAND

LUBEC NARROWS

ROUTE 189 TO US ROUTE 1

TO WEST QUODDY

HEAD HARBOUR PASSAGE

HEAD HARBOUR LIGHT

HEAD HARBOUR I.

WILSONS BEACH

CAMPOBELLO ISLAND
CANADA

DEER ISLAND FERRY

FRIARS BAY

HERRING COVE

LUBEC

SEE INSERT

RACCOON POINT

TIDAL FLATS
MARSH

MILE

N

QUODDY NARROWS

LIBERTY POINT

Chapter 20

Eastport

Deer Island Ferry
Eastport Flats
Eastport Waterfront

Separated from Lubec across Cobscook Bay by less than 3 miles of water (but 40 miles of road) is the city of Eastport. The easternmost city in the United States, Eastport sits on Moose Island in lower Passamaquoddy Bay overlooking Deer Island and Campobello Island, New Brunswick. From a birder's standpoint Eastport has much to offer: the Eastport-Deer Island ferry from which you can see a phenomenal concentration of phalaropes and gulls in late summer; the Eastport flats, which offer some of the best shore-birding in the state; and the Eastport waterfront, which is an excellent spot particularly in winter to look for unusual gulls and alcids. In late summer, when birding is most productive, you can spend the better part of a day here.

Deer Island Ferry

The passages among the islands in Passamaquoddy Bay offer some fine birding, and fortunately two small ferries run between them — one from Eastport to Deer Island and the other from Campobello to Deer Island. From mid-August to mid-September on either one you can see a concentration of Northern Phalaropes in Passamaquoddy Bay that can number in the millions. A phenomenon that John James Audubon noted in 1833 when he stopped in Eastport en route to Labrador, it is no less impressive today. The highest counts, which range from several hundred thousand to two or three million, usually coincide with the extreme tides of the new and full moons, when phalaropes spread like a slick across the water and rise from the horizon like distant clouds of smoke. Thousands of Bonaparte's Gulls also congregate in the channels then, with smaller numbers of Greater Black-backed, Herring, and Ring-billed Gulls. Look also for Little and Black-headed Gulls and possibly something rarer: Franklin's and Sabine's Gulls have been seen from the Deer Island ferries in August and September.

The Eastport-Deer Island ferry runs from early June through September and the Campobello-Deer Island ferry from late June to Labor Day. Although they are best for phalaropes from mid-August on, you can see interesting gulls at any time. Travel from Eastport or Campobello to Deer Island and back. There's no need to take your car, and passenger fare is nominal.

Eastport Flats

Together with the Lubec flats on the other side of Cobscook Bay, Eastport offers some of the best shorebirding in Maine. All along Route 190 from Perry into Eastport you'll see extensive mud flats and gravel bars which attract among the largest concentrations of shorebirds anywhere in Maine. The area is most productive in the fall. Although migration generally peaks in mid-August, it is well worth a visit anytime from mid-July well into the fall. You can work the area easily from the roadside. Half Moon Cove and Carrying Place Cove, 3.5 miles and 5.0 miles south of Route 1, usually are the most productive areas. Also check Perry's Pond, 1.1 miles south of Route 1. This is private property, but you can scan it from the roadside. The best time to work the Eastport flats is either side of high tide and especially on a falling tide. At low tide the birds are too widely dispersed to be seen closely. Regular species you can expect to see at Eastport are Semipalmated and Black-bellied Plovers, Greater and Lesser Yellowlegs, Least and Semipalmated Sandpipers, and Short-billed Dowitchers. As at Lubec, Semipalmated and Least Sandpipers are particularly abundant (the former far more numerous), with counts of 10,000 to 15,000 not uncommon in late July and August. Less common species are Killdeer, Lesser Golden Plover, Willet, Spotted Sandpiper, Ruddy Turnstone, Red Knot, Sanderling, White-rumped and Western Sandpipers, and Dunlin. Piping Plover, Hudsonian and Marbled Godwits, Wilson's Phalarope, Long-billed Dowitcher, and Baird's and Stilt Sandpipers are rare here. Perry's Pond is the most likely place to see a Wilson's Phalarope, and Ruff has also been seen here. The spring species composition in Eastport is similar to that of fall, though no large numbers of any species pass through.

Eastport Waterfront

The Eastport waterfront is worth scanning at any time of year—for small gulls year-round and particularly in late summer and fall, and for white-winged gulls, alcids, and a good variety of waterbirds in winter. Check the town pier and factory wharves along Water Street. From November through March look for loons and grebes, sometimes large numbers of Great Cormorants, common sea ducks, and small numbers of Purple Sandpipers off Eastport. Black-legged Kittiwakes often are abundant offshore. Hard-to-find species which you sometimes can see here are Barrow's Goldeneye, Harlequin Duck, Glaucous, Iceland, and Black-headed Gulls, and all 6 species of alcids. Little Gull has been seen here in summer as well as winter, and this is one of the few places in Maine where Ivory Gull has been seen. At any time of year you might see a Bald Eagle.

Directions

To reach Eastport turn south off Route 1 onto Route 190 in Perry and continue 7.5 miles to Water Street. Turn left and you'll see the town pier on your right almost immediately. The Deer Island Ferry Terminal is 0.2 miles further, next to the big red cannery. From here turn around and come back down Water Street, investigating piers and coves along the way.

Accommodations

The nearest motels, open year-round, are in Calais. There are campgrounds in Perry and at Cobscook Bay State Park.

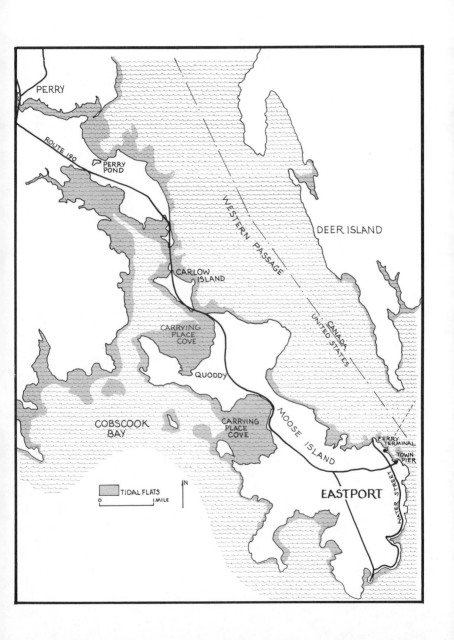

Chapter 21

Moosehorn National Wildlife Refuge

Moosehorn National Wildlife Refuge lies on the Maine-New Brunswick border just south of Calais. Established in 1937 as the northeastern end of a chain of migratory bird refuges from Florida to Maine, it consists of 2 units about 20 miles apart. The northern and primary unit, called the Baring Unit, is the most interesting to birders. Although the refuge is managed to increase habitat for the American Woodcock and waterfowl, you can see a great variety of other birds here as well. More than 200 species have been recorded on the refuge and more than 130 of these have been found nesting, including Spruce Grouse, Black-backed Three-toed Woodpecker, Gray Jay, and 23 species of warblers. The best time to visit is from mid-May through mid-September, when the breeding species are present.

The Baring Unit of Moosehorn consists of 16,000 acres bordered on the north by the St. Croix River. The terrain is highly glaciated and characterized by rolling hills, large ledge outcrops, a few lakes and bogs, and many ponds, marshes, and streams. Virtually the entire natural drainage system of the area has been altered by the Fish & Wildlife Service for waterfowl management purposes. Former meadows and wooded swamps have been flooded to form a myriad of small and large ponds, providing extensive feeding and nesting habitat for species such as Canada Goose, American Black Duck, Green-winged and Blue-winged Teal, Wood Duck, Ring-necked Duck, Common Goldeneye, and Hooded and Common Mergansers. Several other species of waterfowl regularly stop over on migration.

The Baring Unit is primarily an upland area and is forested with second growth stands of aspen, beech, birch, maple, spruce, fir, and pine. Signs of management for the American Woodcock are everywhere, with numerous small clear-cuts distributed virtually throughout the refuge and in various stages of regeneration. If you've never seen a woodcock display, ask at refuge headquarters for directions to a display area. The birds are most active from mid-April to mid-May.

Primary access to the refuge is from the Charlotte Road which runs between Route 1 and Route 214. The visitor center at the intersection of Route 1 and the Charlotte Road gives an excellent overview of the middle section of the Magurrewock Marsh and its stream. It is a good place to observe waterfowl, especially during migration when large numbers of birds stop here. It is also a good spot to see Bald Eagles, which often roost in the trees around the edge, at almost any time of the year. Ospreys are often seen fishing in the open water in spring and summer. The Magurrewock Marsh area, along with many other smaller freshwater marshes on the refuge, provides nesting habitat for many species. Check the marsh, including the lower and upper sections, for Pied-billed Grebe, American Bittern, Virginia Rail, Sora, American Coot, Marsh Wren, Red-winged Blackbird, and Swamp Sparrow. Common Snipe are often seen feeding in the wet areas around the marsh edge, and Sedge Wrens have nested around the marsh some years.

From the visitor center continue 2.5 miles south on the

Charlotte Road to the Headquarters Road. Turn right and continue to the refuge office, where you can pick up a map of the refuge and the bird and mammal lists. The various roads on the refuge cover a variety of habitats. Most of them are open to foot traffic only.

The northern section of the Headquarters Road, the Two-mile Meadow Road, and the Mile Bridge Road traverse a mixture of Red and White Pine, some spruce and Balsam Fir, and a mixture of birches, aspen, beech, and maple. Species you can see here in spring and summer include Goshawk, Sharp-shinned and Cooper's Hawks, Broad-winged Hawk, Ruffed Grouse, Great Horned, Barred, and Saw-whet Owls, Whip-poor-will, Common Flicker, Hairy and Downy Woodpeckers, Great Crested and Least Flycatchers, Eastern Pewee, Northern Raven, American Crow, Black-capped Chickadee, Red-breasted Nuthatch, Brown Creeper, Hermit and Swainson's Thrushes, Golden-crowned and Ruby-crowned Kinglets, Solitary and Red-eyed Vireos, Black-and-white and Nashville Warblers, Northern Parula, Magnolia, Yellow-rumped (Myrtle), and Black-throated Green Warblers, Ovenbird, Canada Warbler, Rose-breasted Grosbeak, Purple Finch, Northern Junco, and White-throated Sparrow.

The South Trail, along with the southern end of the Headquarters Road, the South Ridge Road, and Beaver Trail, offers more extensive stands of second-growth coniferous woods, primarily spruces and firs. The Snare Meadow Road also allows access to primarily spruce-fir habitat, though much of the area here has been logged close to the road. These two areas offer the best opportunities to see permanent resident boreal species such as Spruce Grouse, Black-backed Three-toed Woodpecker, Gray Jay, and Boreal Chickadee. In spring and summer look also for Olive-sided Flycatcher, Cape May, Black-throated Blue, Blackburnian, and Bay-breasted Warblers, in addition to many of the species mentioned above.

The Goodall Heath and Vose Pond area is wooded mostly with birches and aspens near the road, in addition to some mixed woods, and provides good habitat for Philadelphia Vireos.

The many ponds, swamps, and streams on the refuge offer extensive wet edge habitats, primarily overgrown with alders. In spring and summer, these wet thickets and edge areas are good places to look for a variety of species, including Yellow-bellied and Alder Flycatchers, Gray Catbird, Veery, Tennessee and Chestnut-sided Warblers, Northern Waterthrush, Common Yellowthroat, Wilson's Warbler, and American Redstart. Another species to look for in these habitats is Rusty Blackbird. Additionally, extensive stands of dead trees, primarily spruces, in flooded areas are good places to look for Yellow-bellied Sapsucker and Black-backed Three-toed Woodpecker, which often search for food on the dead timber.

True bog habitat is not extensive in the Baring Unit, but areas such as the Goodall Heath and Town Heath are worth checking for nesting Palm Warbler and Lincoln Sparrow.

While walking the trails or driving the Charlotte Road, keep your eyes open for mammals. Beaver are very common on the refuge, and their work is visible on nearly every pond. Porcupines also are seen commonly. Whitetail Deer, Red Fox, Raccoon, and Black Bear are also present, as well as a large number of smaller mammals.

Directions

The visitor center at Moosehorn is 3 miles south of Calais at the intersection of Route 1 and the Charlotte Road. To reach the refuge from the south, turn north off Route 214 in Charlotte onto the Charlotte Road.

Accommodations

Motels are open year-round in Calais. The nearest campground is Cobscook Bay State Park to the south in Whiting.

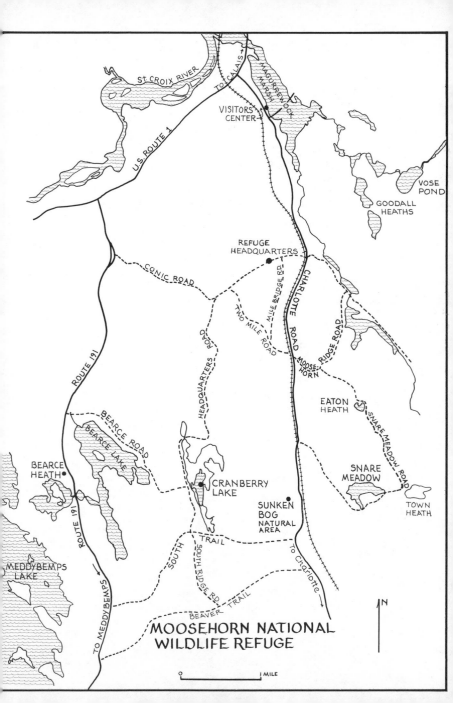

MOOSEHORN NATIONAL
WILDLIFE REFUGE

Appendixes

Appendix A

Terminology

The common and Latin names used in this book follow the American Birding Association Checklist, *Birds of Continental United States and Canada,* first edition, 1975.

The following terms are used to indicate groups of birds:

alcids: Razorbill, Dovekie, Thick-billed and Thin-billed Murres, Atlantic Puffin, Black Guillemot.

landbirds: grouse, hawks, doves, cuckoos, owls, swifts, hummingbirds, kingfishers, woodpeckers, and passerines. (Hawks and owls are often referred to separately as raptors.)

marsh birds: any of several species found in marshes.

passerines: perching birds. Includes all families from flycatchers through sparrows.

"peep": the small sandpipers.

pelagic birds: birds of open ocean. Albatrosses, shearwaters, petrels, gannets, jaegers, skuas, some gulls, and alcids.

raptors: vultures, hawks, eagles, falcons, owls.

shorebirds: oystercatchers, plovers, turnstones, woodcock, snipe, curlews, sandpipers, godwits, avocets, stilts, and phalaropes.

"tubenoses": albatrosses, shearwaters, petrels.

wading birds: herons, egrets, bitterns, ibises.

waterbirds: all swimming birds, including waterfowl.

waterfowl: swans, geese, and ducks.

Appendix B

Birds of the Maine Coast

The following list is intended to provide a general idea of the chances of finding a certain species at different times of year. This is not intended to be an indicator of the relative abundance of each species, nor is it a comprehensive treatise on the birds of the coast. The percentages indicated assume that you are looking in the right habitat (note any letters or an asterisk next to the species name). For example, Spruce Grouse breeds primarily east of Penobscot Bay (bE) and will be seen in the percentages indicated only if you are looking in that area. Some species, such as Winter Wren, are heard far more often that they are seen and will be recorded in the percentages indicated only by observers who are familiar with their songs and calls. Other species, such as owls and rails, may be recorded as indicated only if tapes of their songs or calls are played to attract them.

b	breeds in the state
(b)	probably breeds in the state but not yet confirmed
bW	along the coast breeds primarily west of Penobscot Bay
bE	along the coast breeds primarily east of Penobscot Bay
bI	breeds primarily inland
W	found primarily west of Penobscot Bay
E	found primarily east of Penobscot Bay
I	found primarily inland
*	see Appendix C, Birds of Special Interest

likely to be seen on 100% of trips in the right habitat ━━━

likely to be seen on 75% or more of trips ━━━━━━━━━

likely to be seen on 33% or more of trips ────────

likely to be seen on 10% or more of trips — — — — — — — — —

likely to be seen on less than 10% of trips . . . .

| | | JAN | FEB | MAR | APR | MAY | JUN | JUL | AUG | SEP | OCT | NOV | DEC |

Common Loon* b
    Gavia immer
Red-throated Loon*
    Gavia stellata
Red-necked Grebe*
    Podiceps grisegena
Horned Grebe
    Podiceps auritus
Pied-billed Grebe b
    Podilymbus podiceps
Yellow-nosed Albatross
    Diomedea chlororhynchos
Northern Fulmar*
    Fulmarus glacialis
Cory's Shearwater*
    Puffinus diomedea
Greater Shearwater*
    Puffinus gravis
Sooty Shearwater*
    Puffinus griseus
Manx Shearwater*
    Puffinus puffinus
Leach's Storm Petrel* b
    Oceanodroma leucorhoa
Wilson's Storm Petrel*
    Oceanites oceanicus
Northern Gannet*
    Morus bassanus
Great Cormorant*
    Phalacrocorax carbo
Double-crested Cormorant b
    Phalacrocorax auritus
Great Blue Heron b
    Ardea herodias
Green Heron b
    Butorides striatus
Little Blue Heron* bW
    Florida caerulea
Cattle Egret* bW
    Bubulcus ibis

174

Great Egret*   W
Casmerodius albus

Snowy Egret*   bW
Egretta thula

Louisiana Heron*   bW
Hydranassa tricolor

Black-crowned Night Heron*   b
Nycticorax nycticorax

Yellow-crowned Night Heron
Nyctanassa violacea

Least Bittern*   b
Ixobrychus exilis

American Bittern   b
Botaurus lentiginosus

Glossy Ibis*   bW
Plegadis falcinellus

Mute Swan
Cygnus olor

Whistling Swan
Olor columbianus

Canada Goose   bE
Branta canadensis

Brant*
Branta bernicla

Snow Goose*
Chen caerulescens

Mallard   b
Anas platyrhynchos

American Black Duck   b
Anas rubripes

Gadwall   b
Anas strepera

Common Pintail
Anas acuta

Green-winged Teal   bE
Anas crecca

Blue-winged Teal   bE
Anas discors

Eurasian Wigeon
Anas penelope

175

American Wigeon b
Anas americana

Northern Shoveler b
Anas clypeata

Wood Duck b
Aix sponsa

Redhead
Aythya americana

Ring-necked Duck bE
Aythya collaris

Canvasback
Aythya valisineria

Greater Scaup
Aythya marila

Lesser Scaup
Aythya affinis

Common Goldeneye bE
Bucephala clangula

Barrow's Goldeneye*
Bucephala islandica

Bufflehead
Bucephala albeola

Oldsquaw*
Clangula hyemalis

Harlequin Duck*
Histrionicus histrionicus

Common Eider* b
Somateria mollissima

King Eider*
Somateria spectabilis

White-winged Scoter*
Melanitta deglandi

Surf Scoter*
Melanitta perspicillata

Black Scoter*
Melanitta nigra

Ruddy Duck*
Oxyura jamaicensis

Hooded Merganser* bE
Lophodytes cucullatus

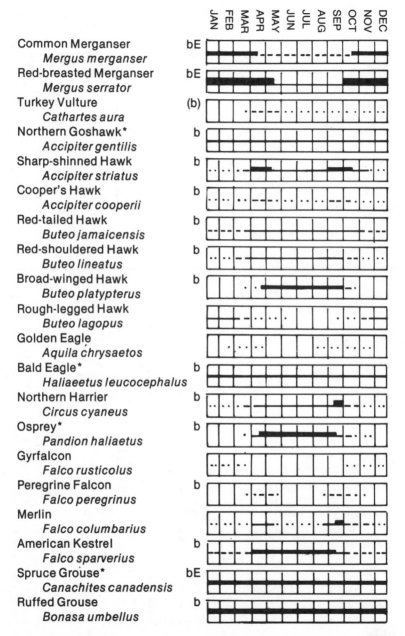

		JAN	FEB	MAR	APR	MAY	JUN	JUL	AUG	SEP	OCT	NOV	DEC
Common Merganser	bE												
Mergus merganser													
Red-breasted Merganser	bE												
Mergus serrator													
Turkey Vulture	(b)												
Cathartes aura													
Northern Goshawk*	b												
Accipiter gentilis													
Sharp-shinned Hawk	b												
Accipiter striatus													
Cooper's Hawk	b												
Accipiter cooperii													
Red-tailed Hawk	b												
Buteo jamaicensis													
Red-shouldered Hawk	b												
Buteo lineatus													
Broad-winged Hawk	b												
Buteo platypterus													
Rough-legged Hawk													
Buteo lagopus													
Golden Eagle													
Aquila chrysaetos													
Bald Eagle*	b												
Haliaeetus leucocephalus													
Northern Harrier	b												
Circus cyaneus													
Osprey*	b												
Pandion haliaetus													
Gyrfalcon													
Falco rusticolus													
Peregrine Falcon	b												
Falco peregrinus													
Merlin													
Falco columbarius													
American Kestrel	b												
Falco sparverius													
Spruce Grouse*	bE												
Canachites canadensis													
Ruffed Grouse	b												
Bonasa umbellus													

177

Species (Scientific name)	Status	JAN	FEB	MAR	APR	MAY	JUN	JUL	AUG	SEP	OCT	NOV	DEC
Ring-necked Pheasant (*Phasianus colchicus*)	b	▬	▬	▬	▬	▬	▬	▬	▬	▬	▬	▬	▬
Sandhill Crane (*Grus canadensis*)						• •	• •	• •	• •	• •	• •		
King Rail (*Rallus elegans*)					•	• •	• •	•	•	•	• •	•	• •
Clapper Rail (*Rallus longirostris*)					•	• •	•			• •	•	• •	•
Virginia Rail (*Rallus limicola*)	b				•	▬▬▬	▬▬▬	▬▬▬	▬▬▬	▬▬	•		
Sora (*Porzana carolina*)	b			•	• —	▬▬▬	▬▬▬	▬▬▬	▬▬▬	▬▬ —	•		
Purple Gallinule (*Porphyrula martinica*)				•	• •	•	•	•	•	•	•	•	• •
Common Gallinule (*Gallinula chloropus*)	b			•	• •	•	•	•	•	•	•		
American Coot (*Fulica americana*)	b	• •	•	• —	• —	—	—	—	—	—	▬▬▬	•	• •
American Oystercatcher (*Haematopus palliatus*)					•	•	•	•	•	•	• •		
American Avocet (*Recurvirostra americana*)					• •		•	•	•	•	•	•	
Semipalmated Plover (*Charadrius semipalmatus*)						███	—	████	████	—	— •	•	
Killdeer (*Charadrius vociferus*)	b	•		•	████	████	████	████	████	████	—	—	• •
Piping Plover* (*Charadrius melodus*)	bW			•	• ▬	▬▬▬	▬▬▬	▬▬▬	▬▬	•			
Lesser Golden Plover* (*Pluvialis dominica*)					• •		•	• —	—	—	• •		
Black-bellied Plover (*Pluvialis squatarola*)					███	███	— •	—	████	████	—	•	• •
Hudsonian Godwit* (*Limosa haemastica*)								• —	— —	— •			
Marbled Godwit (*Limosa fedoa*)								• •	• •				
Whimbrel* (*Numenius phaeopus*)						• •	•	• ▬	▬▬▬	• •			
Upland Sandpiper* (*Bartramia longicauda*)	b				• ▬	▬▬▬	▬▬▬	▬▬▬	▬▬▬	• •			

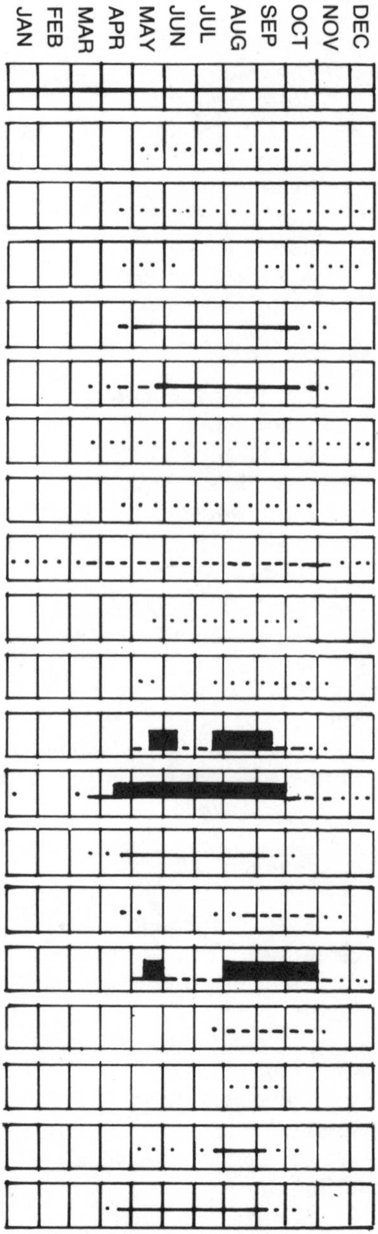

178

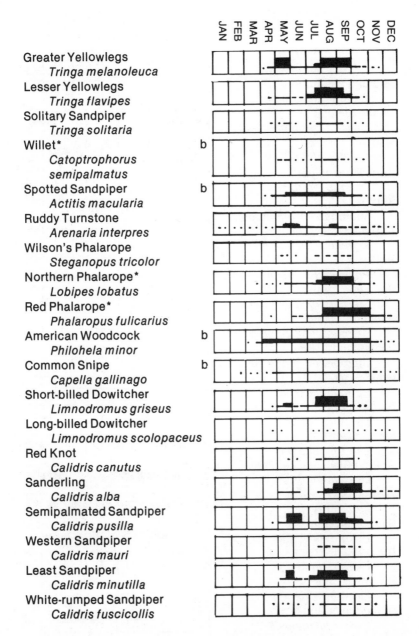

Greater Yellowlegs
Tringa melanoleuca

Lesser Yellowlegs
Tringa flavipes

Solitary Sandpiper
Tringa solitaria

Willet*   b
Catoptrophorus semipalmatus

Spotted Sandpiper   b
Actitis macularia

Ruddy Turnstone
Arenaria interpres

Wilson's Phalarope
Steganopus tricolor

Northern Phalarope*
Lobipes lobatus

Red Phalarope*
Phalaropus fulicarius

American Woodcock   b
Philohela minor

Common Snipe   b
Capella gallinago

Short-billed Dowitcher
Limnodromus griseus

Long-billed Dowitcher
Limnodromus scolopaceus

Red Knot
Calidris canutus

Sanderling
Calidris alba

Semipalmated Sandpiper
Calidris pusilla

Western Sandpiper
Calidris mauri

Least Sandpiper
Calidris minutilla

White-rumped Sandpiper
Calidris fuscicollis

Species		
Baird's Sandpiper	*Calidris bairdii*	
Pectoral Sandpiper	*Calidris melanotos*	
Purple Sandpiper*	*Calidris maritima*	
Dunlin	*Calidris alpina*	
Curlew Sandpiper	*Calidris ferruginea*	
Stilt Sandpiper	*Micropalama himantopus*	
Buff-breasted Sandpiper	*Tryngites subruficollis*	
Ruff	*Philomachus pugnax*	
Pomarine Jaeger	*Stercorarius pomarinus*	
Parasitic Jaeger	*Stercorarius parasiticus*	
Long-tailed Jaeger	*Stercorarius longicaudus*	
Great Skua	*Catharacta skua*	
Glaucous Gull*	*Larus hyperboreus*	
Iceland Gull*	*Larus glaucoides*	
Greater Black-backed Gull	*Larus marinus*	b
Herring Gull	*Larus argentatus*	b
Ring-billed Gull	*Larus delawarensis*	bl
Black-headed Gull	*Larus ridibundus*	
Laughing Gull	*Larus atricilla*	b
Bonaparte's Gull	*Larus philadelphia*	

Little Gull
Larus minutus

Ivory Gull
Pagophila eburnea

Black-legged Kittiwake*
Rissa tridactyla

Sabine's Gull
Xema sabini

Forster's Tern
Sterna fosteri

Common Tern*   b
Sterna hirundo

Arctic Tern*   b
Sterna paradisaea

Roseate Tern*   bW
Sterna dougallii

Little Tern*   bW
Sterna albifrons

Caspian Tern
Sterna caspia

Black Tern*   bI
Chlidonias niger

Razorbill*   b
Alca torda

Thin-billed Murre*
Uria aalge

Thick-billed Murre*
Uria lomvia

Dovekie*
Alle alle

Black Guillemot*   b
Cepphus grylle

Atlantic Puffin*   b
Fratercula arctica

Rock Dove   b
Columba livia

Mourning Dove   b
Zenaida macroura

Yellow-billed Cuckoo   b
Coccyzus americanus

		J A N	F E B	M A R	A P R	M A Y	J U N	J U L	A U G	S E P	O C T	N O V	D E C

Black-billed Cuckoo — b
Coccyzus erythropthalmus

Common Screech Owl
Otus asio

Great Horned Owl — b
Bubo virginianus

Snowy Owl*
Nyctea scandiaca

Hawk Owl
Surnia ulula

Barred Owl — b
Strix varia

Great Gray Owl
Strix nebulosa

Long-eared Owl — b
Asio otus

Short-eared Owl — (b)
Asio flammeus

Boreal Owl
Aegolius funereus

Saw-whet Owl — b
Aegolius acadicus

Whip-poor-will — b
Caprimulgus vociferus

Common Nighthawk — b
Chordeiles minor

Chimney Swift — b
Chaetura pelagica

Ruby-throated Hummingbird — b
Archilochus colubris

Belted Kingfisher — b
Megaceryle alcyon

Common Flicker — b
Colaptes auratus

Pileated Woodpecker — b
Dryocopus pileatus

Red-bellied Woodpecker
Melanerpes carolinus

182

Red-headed Woodpecker
Melanerpes
erythrocephalus

Yellow-bellied Sapsucker   b
Sphyrapicus varius

Hairy Woodpecker   b
Picoides villosus

Downy Woodpecker   b
Picoides pubescens

Black-backed Three-toed
Woodpecker*   bE
Picoides arcticus

Northern Three-toed
Woodpecker*   bE
Picoides tridactylus

Eastern Kingbird   b
Tyrannus tyrannus

Western Kingbird
Tyrannus verticalis

Scissor-tailed Flycatcher
Muscivora forficata

Great Crested Flycatcher   bW
Myiarchus crinitus

Eastern Phoebe   b
Sayornis phoebe

Yellow-bellied Flycatcher*   bE
Empidonax flaviventris

Acadian Flycatcher
Empidonax virescens

Willow Flycatcher*   bW
Empidonax traillii

Alder Flycatcher*   b
Empidonax alnorum

Least Flycatcher   b
Empidonax minimus

Eastern Pewee   b
Contopus virens

Olive-sided Flycatcher*   b
Nuttallornis borealis

Species		Chart
Horned Lark	b	
Eremophila alpestris		
Tree Swallow	b	
Iridoprocne bicolor		
Bank Swallow	b	
Riparia riparia		
Rough-winged Swallow	b	
Stelgidopteryx ruficollis		
Barn Swallow	b	
Hirundo rustica		
Cliff Swallow	b	
Petrochelidon pyrrhonota		
Purple Martin	b	
Progne subis		
Gray Jay*	bE	
Perisoreus canadensis		
Blue Jay	b	
Cyanocitta cristata		
Northern Raven*	bE	
Corvus corax		
American Crow	b	
Corvus brachyrhynchos		
Black-capped Chickadee	b	
Parus atricapillus		
Boreal Chickadee*	bE	
Parus hudsonicus		
Tufted Titmouse	b	
Parus bicolor		
White-breasted Nuthatch	b	
Sitta carolinensis		
Red-breasted Nuthatch	b	
Sitta canadensis		
Brown Creeper	b	
Certhia familiaris		
House Wren	b	
Troglodytes aedon		
Winter Wren*	bE	
Troglodytes troglodytes		
Carolina Wren		
Thryothorus ludovicianus		

184

	JAN	FEB	MAR	APR	MAY	JUN	JUL	AUG	SEP	OCT	NOV	DEC

Marsh Wren — bW
Cistothorus palustris

Sedge Wren — b
Cistothorus platensis

Northern Mockingbird — b
Mimus polyglottos

Gray Catbird — b
Dumetella carolinensis

Brown Thrasher — bW
Toxostoma rufum

American Robin — b
Turdus migratorius

Varied Thrush
Ixoreus naevius

Wood Thrush — bW
Hylocichla mustelina

Hermit Thrush — b
Catharus guttatus

Swainson's Thrush — bE
Catharus ustulatus

Gray-cheeked Thrush* — bI
Catharus minimus

Veery — b
Catharus fuscescens

Eastern Bluebird — b
Sialia sialis

Northern Wheatear
Oenanthe oenanthe

Blue-gray Gnatcatcher* — (b)W
Polioptila caerulea

Golden-crowned Kinglet — b
Regulus satrapa

Ruby-crowned Kinglet — b
Regulus calendula

Water Pipit — bI
Anthus spinoletta

Bohemian Waxwing*
Bombycilla garrulus

Cedar Waxwing — b
Bombycilla cedrorum

185

Northern Shrike*
Lanius excubitor

Loggerhead Shrike   b
Lanius ludovicianus

European Starling   b
Sturnus vulgaris

White-eyed Vireo
Vireo griseus

Yellow-throated Vireo*   bW
Vireo flavifrons

Solitary Vireo   b
Vireo solitarius

Red-eyed Vireo   b
Vireo olivaceus

Philadelphia Vireo*   bE
Vireo philadelphicus

Warbling Vireo   b
Vireo gilvus

Black-and-white Warbler   b
Mniotilta varia

Prothonotary Warbler
Protonotaria citrea

Worm-eating Warbler
Helmitheros vermivorus

Golden-winged Warbler   (b)W
Vermivora chrysoptera

Blue-winged Warbler*   bW
Vermivora pinus

Tennessee Warbler*   bE
Vermivora peregrina

Orange-crowned Warbler
Vermivora celata

Nashville Warbler*   b
Vermivora ruficapilla

Northern Parula Warbler   b
Parula americana

Yellow Warbler   b
Dendroica petechia

Magnolia Warbler*   b
Dendroica magnolia

Cape May Warbler*   bE
     Dendroica tigrina

Black-throated Blue Warbler*   b
     Dendroica caerulescens

Yellow-rumped Warbler   b
     Dendroica coronata

Black-throated Green Warbler*   b
     Dendroica virens

Cerulean Warbler
     Dendroica cerulea

Blackburnian Warbler*   b
     Dendroica fusca

Yellow-throated Warbler
     Dendroica dominica

Chestnut-sided Warbler   b
     Dendroica pensylvanica

Bay-breasted Warbler*   bE
     Dendroica castanea

Blackpoll Warbler*   bE
     Dendroica striata

Pine Warbler   bW
     Dendroica pinus

Prairie Warbler*   bW
     Dendroica discolor

Palm Warbler*   bE
     Dendroica palmarum

Ovenbird   b
     Seiurus aurocapillus

Northern Waterthrush   b
     Seiurus noveboracensis

Louisiana Waterthrush*   bW
     Seiurus motacilla

Kentucky Warbler
     Oporornis formosus

Connecticut Warbler
     Oporornis agilis

Mourning Warbler*   bE
     Oporornis philadelphia

Common Yellowthroat   b
     Geothlypis trichas

187

| | | JAN | FEB | MAR | APR | MAY | JUN | JUL | AUG | SEP | OCT | NOV | DEC |

Yellow-breasted Chat
Icteria virens

Hooded Warbler
Wilsonia citrina

Wilson's Warbler* bE
Wilsonia pusilla

Canada Warbler b
Wilsonia canadensis

American Redstart b
Setophaga ruticilla

House Sparrow b
Passer domesticus

Bobolink b
Dolichonyx oryzivorus

Eastern Meadowlark b
Sturnella magna

Yellow-headed Blackbird
Xanthocephalus xanthocephalus

Red-winged Blackbird b
Agelaius phoeniceus

Orchard Oriole b
Icterus spurius

Northern Oriole b
Icterus galbula

Rusty Blackbird* bE
Euphagus carolinus

Common Grackle b
Quiscalus quiscula

Brown-headed Cowbird b
Molothrus ater

Western Tanager
Piranga ludoviciana

Scarlet Tanager b
Piranga olivacea

Summer Tanager
Piranga rubra

Northern Cardinal b
Cardinalis cardinalis

188

| | | JAN | FEB | MAR | APR | MAY | JUN | JUL | AUG | SEP | OCT | NOV | DEC |

Rose-breasted Grosbeak   b
     Pheucticus ludovicianus

Blue Grosbeak
     Guiraca caerulea

Indigo Bunting   b
     Passerina cyanea

Dickcissel
     Spiza americana

Evening Grosbeak*   bE
     Hesperiphona vespertina

Purple Finch   b
     Carpodacus purpureus

House Finch   b
     Carpodacus mexicanus

Pine Grosbeak*   b
     Pinicola enucleator

Hoary Redpoll
     Carduelis hornemanni

Common Redpoll*
     Carduelis flammea

Pine Siskin*   b
     Carduelis pinus

American Goldfinch   b
     Carduelis tristis

Red Crossbill*   b
     Loxia curvirostris

White-winged Crossbill*   b
     Loxia leucoptera

Rufous-sided Towhee   bW
     Pipilo erythrophthalmus

Savannah Sparrow   b
     Passerculus sandwichensis

Grasshopper Sparrow   bW
     Ammodramus savannarum

Sharp-tailed Sparrow*   b
     Ammospiza caudacuta

Seaside Sparrow
     Ammospiza maritima

Vesper Sparrow   b
     Pooecetes gramineus

189

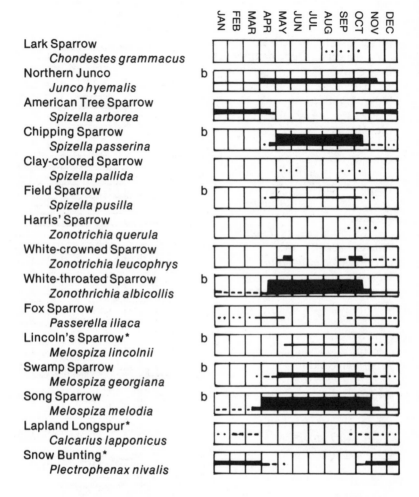

	JAN	FEB	MAR	APR	MAY	JUN	JUL	AUG	SEP	OCT	NOV	DEC

Lark Sparrow
Chondestes grammacus

Northern Junco   b
Junco hyemalis

American Tree Sparrow
Spizella arborea

Chipping Sparrow   b
Spizella passerina

Clay-colored Sparrow
Spizella pallida

Field Sparrow   b
Spizella pusilla

Harris' Sparrow
Zonotrichia querula

White-crowned Sparrow
Zonotrichia leucophrys

White-throated Sparrow   b
Zonothrichia albicollis

Fox Sparrow
Passerella iliaca

Lincoln's Sparrow*   b
Melospiza lincolnii

Swamp Sparrow   b
Melospiza georgiana

Song Sparrow   b
Melospiza melodia

Lapland Longspur*
Calcarius lapponicus

Snow Bunting*
Plectrophenax nivalis

190

The following species occur very rarely in Maine. Those which have not been photographed or collected, or for some other reason have not been verified with absolute confidence, are considered hypothetical.

Arctic Loon	*Gavia arctica*	hypothetical
Eared Grebe	*Podiceps nigricollis*	hypothetical
Western Grebe	*Aechmophorus occidentalis*	
Cape Petrel	*Daption capense*	
Little Shearwater	*Puffinus assimilis*	hypothetical
Audubon's Shearwater	*Puffinus lherminieri*	hypothetical
Black-capped Petrel	*Pterodroma hasitata*	hypothetical
British Storm Petrel	*Hydrobates pelagicus*	hypothetical
White-tailed Tropicbird	*Phaethon lepturus*	
American White Pelican	*Pelecanus erythrorhynchos*	
Brown Pelican	*Pelecanus occidentalis*	
Magnificent Frigatebird	*Fregata magnificens*	
Lesser Frigatebird	*Fregata ariel*	
Wood Stork	*Mycteria americana*	
Whooper Swan	*Olor cygnus*	
Greater White-fronted Goose	*Anser albifrons*	

Fulvous Whistling Duck   *Dendrocygna bicolor*
Steller's Eider   *Polysticta stelleri*
Black Vulture   *Coragyps atratus*
Swainson's Hawk   *Buteo swainsoni*
Willow Ptarmigan   *Lagopus lagopus*
Yellow Rail   *Coturnicops noveboracensis*
Corn Crake   *Crex crex*
Black-necked Stilt   *Himantopus mexicanus*
Northern Lapwing   *Vanellus vanellus*
Bar-tailed Godwit   *Limosa lapponica*
Eskimo Curlew   *Numenius borealis*
Long-billed Curlew   *Numenius americanus*
Rufous-necked Stint   *Calidris ruficollis*
Lesser Black-backed Gull   *Larus fuscus*
Mew Gull   *Larus canus*   hypothetical
Franklin's Gull   *Larus pipixcan*
Gull-billed Tern   *Gelochelidon nilotica*
Sooty Tern   *Sterna fuscata*
Royal Tern   *Sterna maxima*
Sandwich Tern   *Sterna sandvicensis*   hypothetical
Black Skimmer   *Rynchops niger*
Tufted Puffin   *Lunda cirrhata*   hypothetical
Band-tailed Pigeon   *Columba fasciata*
White-winged Dove   *Zenaida asiatica*
Barn Owl   *Tyto alba*
Chuck-will's-widow   *Caprimulgus carolinensis*
Rufous Hummingbird   *Selasphorus rufus*
Tropical Kingbird   *Tyrannus melancholicus*
Fork-tailed Flycatcher   *Muscivora tyrannus*
Variegated Flycatcher   *Empidonomus varius*
Ash-throated Flycatcher   *Myiarchus cinerascens*
Say's Phoebe   *Sayornis saya*
Black-billed Magpie   *Pica pica*
Fish Crow   *Corvus ossifragus*   hypothetical

Bewick's Wren   *Thryomanes bewickii*   hypothetical
Sprague's Pipit   *Anthus spragueii*   hypothetical
Black-throated Gray Warbler   *Dendroica   nigrescens*
                                          hypothetical
Western Meadowlark   *Sturnella neglecta*
Brewer's Blackbird   *Euphagus cyanocephalus* hypothetical
Black-headed Grosbeak   *Pheucticus melanocephalus*
Lazuli Bunting   *Passerina amoena*
Painted Bunting   *Passerina ciris*   hypothetical
Gray-crowned Rosy Finch   *Leucosticte tephrocotis*
Green-tailed Towhee   *Chlorura chlorura*
Lark Bunting   *Calamospiza melanocorys*
Henslow's Sparrow   *Ammodramus henslowii*
Le Conte's Sparrow   *Ammospiza leconteii*
Smith's Longspur   *Calcarius pictus*
Chestnut-collared Longspur   *Calcarius ornatus*

Appendix C

Birds of Special Interest

Common Loon Regular coastal migrant and winter visitor, when it is more common along the western coast than the eastern. Common breeder inland and local breeder in coastal lakes and ponds east of Penobscot Bay. Non-breeders are found in coastal waters during summer.

Red-throated Loon Regular coastal migrant and winter visitor, often with Common Loon but in smaller numbers. Highest winter concentrations are found in the Reid State Park/Popham Beach area.

Red-necked Grebe Regular coastal migrant and winter visitor. Often forms large offshore rafts at Reid State Park, Otter Point (Mount Desert Island), and other sites.

Northern Fulmar Seen regularly on pelagic trips throughout the year.

Cory's Shearwater A warm-water species found irregularly in the Gulf of Maine. Exceptional summers such as those of 1979 and 1980 brought regular reports of this species from the *Bluenose* and other pelagic trips.

Greater Shearwater Common to abundant summer and early fall visitor, usually seen from the *Bluenose* and on other pelagic trips June through October. Generally the most common shearwater in the Gulf of Maine.

Sooty Shearwater Uncommon to common summer visitor and the second most common shearwater in the Gulf of Maine. Likely to be seen from the *Bluenose* and on other pelagic trips June through September.

Manx Shearwater   Summer visitor in small numbers to the Gulf of Maine, primarily June through September. Recently found nesting in Newfoundland and, on one occasion, in Massachusetts. Reports of birds seemingly nest prospecting in Muscongus Bay and off Bailey Island suggest that this species should be looked for as a possible breeder on coastal islands in Maine in the near future.

Leach's Storm Petrel   Locally distributed breeder on offshore islands such as Machias Seal, Matinicus Seal, Great Duck, Little Duck, Matinicus Rock. Seen regularly from the *Bluenose* June through mid-October. Rare on other pelagic trips farther south.

Wilson's Storm Petrel   Common to abundant summer visitor and the most common "tubenose" summering in the Gulf of Maine. Easily seen from the *Bluenose* and on other pelagic trips June through September.

Northern Gannet   Common offshore migrant in spring and fall, though it generally can be found by experienced observers at almost any time of year (only exceptionally in January and February). Scan the horizon for this species, especially after strong easterly winds, from any place that affords a good view of open ocean.

Great Cormorant   Easily found winter visitor, usually present from late September to early April (Quoddy Head, Schoodic Point, Reid State Park, and other spots). Overlaps with Double-crested Cormorant in fall and spring. Summer cormorants should be checked carefully as small numbers of immature Great Cormorants regularly linger along the coast.

Southern wading birds   Four southern species, Little Blue Heron, Cattle Egret, Louisiana Heron, and Glossy Ibis, have recently expanded their ranges northward and are breeders on islands in west coastal Maine north to Portland (see Wood Island). Additionally, Great Egret, which is not known to breed in the state, is seen regularly in small numbers in the summer in Maine. These 5 species are most often found at Scarborough Marsh and Biddeford Pool.

Snowy Egret   Locally common breeder on offshore islands in west coastal Maine (Wood Island, Appledore Island, and others). This species may breed in Casco Bay and in small numbers further east (Addison). Regularly seen in summer in bays and marshes in west coastal Maine. Less regular east of Casco Bay.

Black-crowned Night Heron   Summer resident. No longer common. Most reports come during August (see chapter 2, Wood Island).

Least Bittern   This elusive species is reported occasionally during summer. May be more common than records indicate due to oversight. Look for it in freshwater marshes with dense vegetation, especially cattails, such as the one at Sherman Lake (see chapter 10, Damariscotta Region).

Brant   Generally an uncommon early spring and late fall migrant along the coast. Good concentrations are seen in the Lubec area.

Snow Goose   Locally common migrant, particularly in spring. Flocks regularly seen in March and April at Scarborough Marsh and on Merrymeeting Bay.

Barrow's Goldeneye   Regular winter visitor in small numbers to open fresh water, bays, and estuaries. Scan all goldeneye flocks carefully, including females. Most easily found on the Penobscot River near the bridge at Bucksport (where a high count of 70 was recently made) and around Mackworth Island (see chapter 5, Portland).

Oldsquaw   Common visitor along the coast November through April.

Harlequin Duck   The best spot for this winter visitor is off Isle au Haut, where the highest New England winter concentrations are usually reported. On the mainland try Cape Neddick, Scarborough Beach State Park, and Checkly Point (see chapter 4, Prout's Neck), and during some years Campobello Island.

Common Eider   Abundant year-round along the coast. Nests on undisturbed coastal islands. Large flocks pass offshore during spring and fall migration. The largest winter concentrations are usually found in the Mount Desert Island/Schoodic peninsula region and in Casco Bay.

King Eider   Reported in small numbers each winter (rarely in summer), usually with flocks of Common Eiders. As with Barrow's Goldeneye, check the females carefully also. A patient eye and familiarity with Common Eiders will usually yield this species for the Maine winter birder who spends any reasonable amount of time searching for Kings.

Scoters   Abundant spring and fall migrants along the coast, where large flocks can be seen passing offshore. All 3 species winter along the coast, with White-winged Scoters generally the most common species east of Casco Bay and

Black Scoters the most common in Casco Bay and westward. Nonbreeding summer birds are locally regular along the coast (Small Point, Stockton Springs, and other spots.)

Ruddy Duck   Rare to uncommon fall migrant and winter visitor. Recently found in small numbers at Stockton Springs November to April.

Hooded Merganser   Fairly common spring and fall migrant. Uncommon breeder in inland Maine and in small numbers on freshwater ponds along the coast. Winters in small numbers on open fresh and brackish water along the coast. Regularly found at Damariscotta Mills (see chapter 10, Damariscotta Region). Also check near the Georgetown Post Office (see chapter 9, Reid State Park), the New Meadows River (see chapter 6, Brunswick Region), on the Babson Brook outlet near the intersection of routes 198 and 102 on Mount Desert Island, and near the intersection of routes 1 and 189 in Whiting.

Northern Goshawk   Regularly seen uncommon permanent resident. Generally nests in White Pine stands near water in west coastal Maine and in conifers and birches in east coastal Maine.

Bald Eagle   Permanent resident, more common along the coast in winter. As of 1979 there were 52 known breeding pairs in the state. Regularly seen at Merrymeeting Bay and around Damariscotta Lake (see chapter 10, Damariscotta Region), and from Mount Desert Island eastward (Mount Desert Island, Jonesport, Machias Bay, Moosehorn National Wildlife Refuge).

Osprey   Common migrant along the coast from mid to late April and in September. Uncommon to locally common breeder along the coast, most often on offshore islands. Easily seen April through September. Can be seen at close range at Wolfe Neck State Park in Freeport, where a nest has been active for many years, and, if you have a canoe or a boat, in many of the island-studded bays from Casco Bay eastward.

Peregrine Falcon   This species was found nesting again in Maine in 1980 for the first time in over 20 years. Details are withheld to protect the birds.

Spruce Grouse   Uncommon to common permanent resident of spruce woods. Look for this species in its preferred habitat from the Schoodic peninsula eastward (Schoodic Point; within 1 mile of Route 1 on Route 187 between Jonesboro and Jonesport; along Route 191 between E. Machias and Cutler; Quoddy Head State Park; Moosehorn National Wildlife Refuge).

Piping Plover   Uncommon breeder along sandy beaches from Wells to Reid State Park. Nests in small numbers at Reid State Park, Popham Beach, Seawall Beach (see chapter 8, Morse Mountain Preserve), Ferry Beach on Prout's Neck, and Drake's Island in Wells. If you walk the sandy beaches in Maine in June and July, please stay as close to the water line as possible. These plovers will leave their nests unattended and exposed to sun and predators in their attempts to distract you from their nest or young.

Lesser Golden Plover   Rare but regular fall migrant, mid-August through October. Look for it particularly in the Eastport/Lubec region and Biddeford Pool.

Hudsonian Godwit   Rare but regular fall migrant. Seen in small numbers each fall at Scarborough Marsh, Ferry Beach on Prout's Neck, Pine Point, Back Cove in Portland, and Biddeford Pool.

Whimbrel   Rare spring and uncommon fall migrant. Seen regularly during fall migration at Biddeford Pool, Little Machias Bay (see chapter 18, Machias Bay Region), Lubec, and on the blueberry barrens near the coast between Cherryfield and Lubec.

Upland Sandpiper   Uncommon spring and fall migrant, found regularly at Back Cove (see chapter 5, Portland). Breeds on the Deblois blueberry barrens.

Willet   Regular coastal migrant in small numbers. Breeds at Scarborough Marsh, where it can be seen regularly from early May to early September.

Northern Phalarope   Common to abundant spring migrant and abundant fall migrant. Regularly seen on pelagic trips from late May through early October, with the largest number occuring from mid-July through September (see chapters 19, Lubec, and 20, Eastport). Another large concentration occurs near Mount Desert Rock in August and September.

Red Phalarope   Uncommon to common spring migrant and common to abundant fall migrant in offshore waters. Seen most commonly from the *Bluenose* and on other pelagic trips from mid-July through October.

Purple Sandpiper   Locally common in winter, favoring rocky shores and islets. Feeds at the edge of the surf on rocks covered with mats of Rockweed (Fucus) and Knotted Wrack (Ascophyllum). Seen from November to April at many spots including Fletcher Neck, Reid State Park, Otter Point (Mount Desert Island), and Quoddy Head State Park.

Glaucous Gull   Regular winter visitor in small numbers from November through March. Most easily found among large concentrations of Greater Black-backed and Herring Gulls.

Iceland Gull   Regular winter visitor, generally much more numerous than Glaucous Gull, also found November through March. Like Glaucous Gull, found most easily among large concentrations of Greater Black-backed and Herring Gulls (harbors, piers, canning factories, dumps).

Black-legged Kittiwake   Most often seen on pelagic trips from September through April. In winter, can also be found in large numbers in the Eastport and Lubec areas and in much smaller numbers off Schoodic Point.

Common Tern   Common in summer along the entire coast. Breeds on offshore islands. The most likely tern to be seen from the mainland.

Arctic Tern   Breeds on offshore islands, with numbers increasing from uncommon to common eastward along the coast. Generally feeds farther offshore than Common Tern. (see chapter 2, Fletcher Neck; chapter 8, Popham Beach State Park/Morse Mountain Preserve; chapter 18, Machias Seal Island.)

Roseate Tern   Breeds in small numbers on offshore islands along the coast. From the mainland most easily seen at Biddeford Pool and Fletcher Neck and from Fort Popham (Popham Beach State Park).

Little Tern   Breeds in small numbers in scattered colonies on sandy beaches from Wells to Phippsburg. Usually seen each year at Wells Harbor, Ferry Beach on Prout's Neck, Seawall Beach (Morse Mountain Preserve), and Popham Beach.

Black Tern   Breeds at 4 inland localities, including Messalonskee Lake in Belgrade, Carlton Pond in Troy, and Douglas Pond in Palmyra. Rarely seen as a migrant along the coast.

Razorbill   Uncommon breeder on offshore islands, where it is most easily found in summer at 2 of its colonies, Machias Seal Island and Matinicus Rock. Small numbers winter along the coast. Locally common in the Eastport region and Grand Manan Channel in early winter (especially December).

Thin-billed Murre   Most easily seen in summer on Machias Seal Island, where a few nonbreeders spend June and July. From November through March this species is best seen on pelagic trips and ferry crossings. Difficult to find in winter from the mainland, and not seen from there in the summer.

Thick-billed Murre   Winter visitor, uncommon along the coast from November through March when it can be seen from many spots (see chapter 20, Eastport). Best seen on winter pelagic trips or ferry crossings such as the one to Monhegan.

Dovekie   Uncommon to common migrant and winter visitor, most easily seen November through March on pelagic trips and ferry crossings (Monhegan, Vinalhaven, and others). Seen from the coast in small numbers each winter, mostly in December and January, from various localities including Eastport, Mount Desert Island, Owl's Head, and Vinalhaven.

Black Guillemot　　　Fairly common permanent resident along rocky coasts. Breeds on offshore islands.

Atlantic Puffin　　　Easily found in June and July at breeding colonies on Machias Seal Island and Matinicus Rock. Attempts are being made to re-establish the species on a former breeding island in Muscongus Bay. Good numbers are seen from the *Bluenose* in August. Pelagic trips and ferry crossings are your best bet in winter, when this species is rarely seen from the mainland.

Snowy Owl　　　A winter visitor subject to incursions and therefore highly variable in numbers from year to year. Seen in open areas, including marshes, fields, and open offshore islands.

Black-backed Three-toed Woodpecker　　　Uncommon permanent resident from Mount Desert Island eastward along the coast (Mount Desert Island, Schoodic Point, within 1 mile of Route 1 on Route 187 between Jonesboro and Jonesport, Quoddy Head State Park, Moosehorn National Wildlife Refuge). Found in spruce-fir stands, where it chips off thin layers of bark, leaving bare, reddish-brown patches on the trunks. Associated with burned and flooded areas and stands of decaying timber. Subject to winter incursions, when it is seen in small numbers west of Mount Desert Island.

Northern Three-toed Woodpecker　　　Seen only occasionally along the extreme eastern coast. Wandering winter birds are rarely seen farther west along the coast. Habitat similar to that of Black-backed Three-toed Woodpecker.

Yellow-bellied Flycatcher   Mainly associated with conifers, or conifers mixed with birches and alders, and with freshwater marshes and bogs and other areas with wet or swampy ground (Seawall Bog on Mount Desert Island, Schoodic Point, Moosehorn National Wildlife Refuge).

Willow Flycatcher   Uncommon summer resident, almost exclusively in extreme southwestern Maine (Brownfield, Eliot, Berwick), in bushy thickets. Reportedly breeding in summers of 1979 and 1980 in East Machias.

Alder Flycatcher   Common breeder along the coast in suitable habitat of alders and bushy thickets.

Olive-sided Flycatcher   Fairly common migrant; fairly common breeder in mature coniferous woods along the coast.

Gray Jay   Uncommon permanent resident of coniferous woods, primarily east of Mount Desert Island along the coast. Often will allow close approach.

Northern Raven   Permanent resident, fairly common east of the Casco Bay region. Uncommon in the Casco Bay region and rare further west and south. Especially favors dumps in winter.

Boreal Chickadee   Uncommon to locally common permanent resident of spruce-fir woods, primarily from Mount Desert Island eastward. Generally much quieter and more shy than the Black-capped, with which it often associates. Can be seen at Mount Desert Island, Schoodic Point, Machias Bay area, Quoddy Head State Park, and Moosehorn National Wildlife Refuge. In winter seen in small numbers in central and west coastal Maine.

Winter Wren Fairly common migrant and breeder, much more often heard than seen. Favors thick undergrowth in damp coniferous woods, but also seen in deciduous areas on migration.

Gray-cheeked Thrush Breeds on inland mountains; not often seen along the coast except on migration.

Blue-gray Gnatcatcher Uncommonly seen migrant and summer visitor. Most reports come from Casco Bay westward. Believed to be breeding in York County.

Bohemian Waxwing Irregular winter visitor to Bangor/Orono region and other inland localities. Not often seen along the coast.

Northern Shrike Irregular winter visitor, varying from uncommon to scarce from year to year. Often perches on tops of trees or dead snags in and around open areas.

Yellow-throated Vireo Breeds in southwestern Maine north to Augusta. Rarely seen along the coast.

Philadelphia Vireo Uncommon migrant and breeder. Favors aspens, alders, maples, birches, and other deciduous trees for nesting.

Blue-winged Warbler First confirmed breeding in the state in 1980 in South Berwick in extreme southwestern Maine. Most reports are from the west coastal area.

Tennessee Warbler Uncommon migrant; uncommon breeder, chiefly from Mount Desert Island eastward. Prefers larch and alder bogs, swamps, and forest clearings. Look for it on Mount Desert Island, Schoodic Point, and at Moosehorn National Wildlife Refuge.

Nashville Warbler Common migrant; fairly common breeder throughout the state in Gray Birches and other deciduous trees at the edge of clearings.

Magnolia Warbler Common migrant in both deciduous and coniferous woods. Common breeder in stands of young spruce and other conifers.

Cape May Warbler Uncommon spring and common fall migrant, seen in various habitats. Uncommon breeder in mature spruces, primarily from Mount Desert Island eastward.

Black-throated Blue Warbler Uncommon to common migrant and breeder in mixed woods.

Black-throated Green Warbler Very common migrant and breeder, both in coniferous and mixed woods.

Blackburnian Warbler Fairly common migrant and breeder, favoring tall spruces, hemlocks, and firs.

Bay-breasted Warbler Uncommon spring and common fall migrant. Uncommon breeder in tall spruces, hemlocks, and firs, primarily along the eastern portion of the coast.

Blackpoll Warbler Uncommon to common migrant and rare to uncommon breeder in spruce woods from Mount Desert Island eastward.

Prairie Warbler   Breeder in the extreme southwestern part of the state, primarily York County, where it frequents Pitch Pines and shrubby areas.

Palm Warbler   Common migrant; common breeder in bogs, primarily from Mount Desert Island eastward (see chapter 14, Mount Desert Island). Also found in The Heath in Old Orchard Beach.

Louisiana Waterthrush   First confirmed breeding in Maine in the summer of 1980, when nests were found in Oxford and York counties. Prefers the vicinity of brooks and streams in damp woods. (see chapter 1, Wells).

Mourning Warbler   Uncommon migrant and uncommon breeder in young growth of recently clear-cut or burned areas, primarily in the northern half of the state.

Wilson's Warbler   Fairly common migrant; fairly common breeder in alder swales, primarily from Mount Desert Island eastward. (see chapter 21, Moosehorn National Wildlife Refuge).

Rusty Blackbird   Fairly common migrant; uncommon breeder in wooded swamps in northern and extreme eastern Maine. Along the coast look for this species in Washington County.

Evening Grosbeak   Common winter visitor along the entire coast. Uncommon to common in east coastal Maine in summer.

Pine Grosbeak   Irregular winter visitor to a variety of habitats, including coniferous, mixed, and deciduous woods, and orchards. Varies from scarce in some years to common in others.

Common Redpoll   Irregular winter visitor, nearly absent in some years and common in others. Frequents weedy fields, marshes, alders, birches, and feeders.

Pine Siskin   Irregular winter visitor and breeder, varying from scarce to abundant. Timing of nesting can vary from late winter to late summer.

Red and White-winged Crossbills   Both species are irregular winter visitors and breeders, highly variable both in number and season from year to year and in breeding location and timing. Most likely to be seen in conifers from Casco Bay eastward.

Sharp-tailed Sparrow   Common migrant, especially in fall, and common breeder in salt marshes.

Lincoln's Sparrow   Uncommon to common migrant, and uncommon breeder, primarily in bogs, from Mount Desert Island eastward (see chapter 14, Mount Desert Island).

Lapland Longspur   Relatively rare fall migrant and winter visitor, seen most often in weedy areas and along sandy beaches. Associates with Horned Larks and Snow Buntings.

Snow Bunting   Winter visitor, varying from rare in some years to common in others. Frequents weedy fields, coastal marshes, sandy beaches, and coastal islands.

Appendix D

Marine Mammals/Coastal Flora

Any pelagic trip in Maine provides a fine opportunity to see whales and seals as well as seabirds. The following list is adapted from *A Field Guide to the Whales and Seals of the Gulf of Maine* by Steve Katona, David Richardson, and Robin Hazard, second edition, College of the Atlantic, Bar Harbor, Me., 1977.

WHALES

Common

Harbor Porpoise	*Phocoena phocoena*
Pothead (Pilot Whale)	*Globicephala melaena*
Finback Whale	*Baleanoptera physalus*
Minke Whale	*Baleanoptera acutorostrata*
Humpback Whale	*Megaptera novaeangliae*

Occasional

White-sided Dolphin	*Lagenorhynchos acutus*
White-beaked Dolphin	*Lagenorhynchos albirostris*
Saddleback Dolphin	*Delphinis delphis*
Killer Whale	*Orcinus orca*
Right Whale	*Eubalaena glacialis*

Rare

Bottlenose Dolphin	*Tursiops truncatus*
Gray Grampus	*Grampus griseus*
Striped Dolphin	*Stenella coeruleoalba*
Beluga	*Delphinapteras leucas*
Sei Whale	*Balaenoptera borealis*
Blue Whale	*Balaenoptera musculus*
Sperm Whale	*Physeter catodon*
Pygmy Sperm Whale	*Kogia breviceps*
Northern Bottlenose Whale	*Hyperodon ampullatus*
True's Beaked Dolphin	*Mesoplodon mirus*
Dense-beaked Whale	*Mesoplodon densirostris*

SEALS

Common
Harbor Seal   *Phoca vitulina*

Occasional
Gray Seal   *Halichoerus grypus*

Rare
Harp Seal   *Pagophilus groenlandicus*
Hooded Seal   *Cystophora cristata*
Walrus   *Odobenus rosmarus*

Coastal Flora

The following are the scientific names of plant species mentioned in this book.

SEAWEEDS
Knotted Wrack   *Ascophyllum nodosum*
Rockweeds   *Fucus* species

LICHENS, MOSSES, AND FUNGI
Earth Star Puffball   *Gaester hygrometricus*
Reindeer Moss   *Cladonia tenuis, alpestris,* and *rangiferina*
Sphagnum Moss   *Sphagnum* species

SEED PLANTS
Alder   *Alnus.* species
American Beach Grass   *Ammophila breviligulata*
American Beech   *Fagus grandifolia*

Arethusa   *Arethusa bulbosa*
Aspens   *Populus* species
Atlantic White Cedar   *Chamaecyparis thyoides*
Balsam Fir   *Abies balsamea*
Bayberry   *Myrica pensylvanicum*
Beach Heather   *Hudsonia tormentosa*
Beach Pea   *Lathyrus maritimus*
Black Grass   *Juncus gerardi*
Black Spruce   *Picea mariana*
Birches   *Betula* species
Bulrush   *Scirpus validus*
Bunchberry   *Cornus canadensis*
Calapogon   *Calapogon puchellus*
Cattails   *Typha* species
Choke Cherry   *Prunus virginiana*
Clintonia   *Clintonia borealis*
Cloudberry   *Rubus chamaemorus*
Common Ragweed   *Ambrosia artemisiifolia*
Common Wood Sorrel   *Oxalis montana*
Dusty Miller   *Artemisia stelleriana*
Eastern Hemlock   *Tsuga canadensis*
Glassworts   *Salicornia* species
Goldenrods   *Solidago* species
Goldthread   *Coptis groenlandica*
Gray Birch   *Betula populifolia*
Jointweed   *Polygonella articulata*
Labrador Tea   *Ledum groenlandicum*
Late Lowbush Blueberry   *Vaccinium angustifolium*
Leatherleaf   *Chamaedaphne calyculata*
Maples   *Acer* species
Mountain Ash   *Pyrus americana*
Mountain Maple   *Acer spicatum*
Oaks   *Quercus* species
Orach   *Atriplex patula*
Pitch Pine   *Pinus rigida*
Pitcher Plant   *Sarracenia purpurea*
Poplars   *Populus* species

Red Raspberry   *Rubus idaeus*
Red Pine   *Pinus resinota*
Red Spruce   *Picea rubens*
Rugosa Rose   *Rosa rugosa*
Salt-Meadow Cord Grass   *Spartina alterniflora*
Salt-meadow Grass   *Spartina patens*
Sea Lavender   *Limonium carolinianum*
Seaside Goldenrod   *Solidago sempervirens*
Seaside Plantain   *Plantago oliganthos*
Sedges   *Carex* species
Shadbush   *Amelanchier* species
Sheep Laurel   *Kalmia angustifolium*
Spike Grass   *Distichlis spicata*
Star Flower   *Trientalis borealis*
Striped Maple   *Acer pensylvanicum*
Sundews   *Drosera* species
Tall Wormwood   *Artemisia caudata*
Tamarack   *Larix laricina*
Trailing Yew   *Taxus canadensis*
Twinflower   *Linnaea borealis*
Viburnums   *Viburnum* species
White Pine   *Pinus strobus*
White Spruce   *Picea glauca*
Willows   *Salix* species
Witch Hazel   *Hamamelis virginiana*

Appendix E

Resources

The following resources should prove helpful to anyone birding on the Maine coast.

BIRD BOOKS

Bond, James, *Native Birds of Mount Desert Island,* second revised edition, Academy of Natural Sciences of Philadelphia (19th Street and the Parkway, Philadelphia, PA 19103), 1971.

Finch, Davis, Russell, William C., and Thompson, Edward V., *Pelagic Birds in the Gulf of Maine,* National Audubon Society (950 Third Avenue, New York, NY 10022), 1978. (Reprinted from *American Birds,* March 1978, vol. 32, no. 2, pp. 140-155 and May 1978, vol. 32, no. 3, pp. 281-294.)

Harrison, Hal H., *A Field Guide to the Birds' Nests in the United States East of the Mississippi River* (Number 21 in the Peterson Field Guide Series), Houghton Mifflin Company, Boston, MA 1975.

Palmer, Ralph S., *Maine Birds,* Bulletin of the Museum of Comparative Zoology, Harvard College (Cambridge, MA 02138), 1949.

Peterson, Roger Tory, *A Field Guide to the Birds East of the Rockies,* fourth edition, Houghton Mifflin Company, Boston, MA, 1980.

Pettingill, Olin Sewall, Jr., editor, *The Bird Watcher's America,* Thomas Y. Crowell Company, New York, NY, 1965.

————, *A Guide to Bird Finding East of the Mississippi,* second edition, Oxford University Press, New York, NY, 1977.

Pough, Richard H., *Audubon Land Bird* Guide, Doubleday and Company, Inc., Garden City, New York, 1946, 1949.

————, *Audubon Water Bird Guide,* Doubleday and Company, Inc., Garden City, New York, 1951.

OTHER NATURAL HISTORY GUIDES

Appollonio, Spencer, *The Gulf of Maine,* Courier of Maine Books, (One Park Drive, Rockland, ME), 1979.

Burt, William H. and Grossenheider, Richard P., *A Field Guide to the Mammals* (Number 5 in the Peterson Field Guide Series), third edition, Houghton Mifflin Company, Boston, MA, 1976.

Dwelley, Marilyn J., *Spring Wildflowers of New England,* Down East Enterprise, Inc., Camden, ME, 1973.

————, *Summer and Fall Wildflowers of New England,* Down East Enterprise, Inc., Camden, ME, 1977.

————, *Trees and Shrubs of New England,* Down East Enterprise, Inc., Camden, ME, 1980.

Edey, Maitland A. and the editors of Time-Life Books, *The Northeast Coast,* The American Wilderness, Time-Life Books, New York, NY, 1972.

Gosner, Kenneth L., *A Field Guide to the Atlantic Seashore* (Number 24 in the Peterson Field Guide Series), Houghton Mifflin Company, Boston, MA, 1979.

Jorgensen, Neil, *A Guide to New England's Landscape,* Pequot Press, Chester, CT, 1977.

Katona, Steve, Richardson, David, and Hazard, Robin, *A Field Guide to the Whales and Seals of the Gulf of Maine,* second edition, College of the Atlantic (Bar Harbor, ME 04609), 1977.

Miller, Dorcas S., *The Maine Coast: A Nature Lover's Guide,* East Woods Press, 820 East Boulevard, Charlotte, NC, 1979.

Newcomb, Lawrence, *Newcomb's Wildflower Guide,* Little, Brown, and Company, Boston, MA and Toronto, Canada, 1977.

Perry, John and Perry, Jane Greverus, *The Random House Guide to Natural Areas of the Eastern United States,* Random House, New York, NY, 1980.

Peterson, Roger Tory and McKenny, Margaret, *A Field Guide to Wildflowers of Northeastern and Northcentral North America,* Houghton Mifflin Company, Boston, MA, 1968.

PERIODICALS

American Birds, published six times a year by the National Audubon Society (950 Third St., New York, NY 10022). Includes regional reports from the U.S. and Canada and articles on field identification. Refer especially to the Northeastern Maritime Region report.

Birding, published six times a year by the American Birding Association (Box 4335, Austin, TX 78765). Articles on a wide variety of subjects, including field identification and bird finding.

The Guillemot, an amateur bi-monthly newsletter published by the Sorrento Scientific Society (Box 373, Sorrento, ME 04677) concerning natural history in Maine.

Maine Bird Life, a quarterly publication edited by Michael K. Lucey, Box 280, RFD #3, Bangor, ME 04401. Primarily a compilation of statewide records.

RECORDS

A Field Guide to Bird Song of Eastern and Central North America (arranged to accompany Roger Tory Peterson's *A Field Guide to the Birds).* Houghton Mifflin Company, Boston, MA, 1971.

Warblers: Songs of Warblers of Eastern North America, Vol. 4 in the Sounds of Nature Series, published by the Federation of Ontario Naturalists. Available in the U.S. from Houghton Mifflin Company, Boston, MA.

MISCELLANEOUS

Maine Bird Alert, Maine Audubon Society
Gilsland Farm
Old Route 1
Falmouth, ME 04105
(207) 781-2330

Appendix F

Campgrounds

The following list is adapted from the "Maine Guide to Camping 1980" (available from Maine Publicity Bureau, 97 Winthrop Street, Hallowell, ME 04347). It is far from a complete list, as innumerable campgrounds are not listed in the guide. Most of these are well marked by roadside signs, though, so finding a campground usually is not a problem.

BAR HARBOR

Acadia National Park, RFD #1, Box 1, Bar Harbor 04609
(207) 288-3338
Hadley's Point Campground, RFD #1, Box 45, Bar Harbor
04609   (207) 288-4808
Mount Desert Campground, Route 198P, Mt. Desert 04660
(207) 244-3710
Mount Desert Narrows Campground, Route 3, Bar Harbor
04609   (207) 288-4782

BIDDEFORD

Red Barn Farm Campground, Biddeford 04005   (207) 284-4282

CAMDEN

Camden Hills State Park, Camden 04843   (207) 236-2890

CAMPOBELLO ISLAND, NEW BRUNSWICK

Roosevelt International Park, Campobello Is., New Brunswick
(506) 752-2922

DAMARISCOTTA

Lake Pemaquid Camping, Damariscotta 04543   (207) 563-5202
Sherman Lake View Camping Area, Route 1, Newcastle 04553
(207) 563-3239

DEER ISLE

Range 7, P.O. Box 12, Deer Isle 04627   (207) 348-6082

ELLSWORTH
Branch Lake Camping Area, Route 1A, Ellsworth 04605
(207) 667-5174
The Gatherings, RFD 3, Box CM, Ellsworth 04605
(207) 667-8826
Patten Pond KOA, Route 1, Box 240A, Brewer 04412

FREEPORT
Recompense Shore Campsites, Freeport 04032
Sandy Cedar Haven, Baker Road, Freeport 04032
Winslow Memorial Park, Staples Point Road, Freeport 04032

GARDINER
Gardiner/Richmond KOA, Route 201, Gardiner 04345
(207) 582-5086

JONESBORO
Sunkhaze Campground, Route 1, Jonesboro 04648
(207) 434-2542

NOBLEBORO
Duck Puddle Campground, Nobleboro 04555   (207) 563-5608
Town Line Shores, RFD 1, Waldoboro 04572   (207) 832-7055

ORR'S ISLAND
Orr's Island Campground, RR Box 65B, Orr's Island 04066
(207) 833-7350

PERRY
Sunrise Shores, Box 47P, Perry 04667   (207) 853-6608

POPHAM BEACH
Ocean View Park, Route 209, Popham Beach 04562
(207) 389-2564

ROCKPORT
Megunticook-by-the-Sea, U.S. Route 1, Rockport 04856
(207) 594-2428

SCARBORO

Wild Duck Camping Area, Dunstan Landing Rd., Scarboro 04074

Bailey's Campground, Ross Road, Pine Point 04074 (207) 883-6043

SMALL POINT

Hermit Island, Small Point 04567   (207) 443-2101

Head Beach Camping Grounds, Small Point 04567

STEUBEN

Mainayr Campground, Steuben 04680   (207) 546-2690

THOMASTON

Atticus Hill Farm, Thomaston 04861   (207) 354-2393

Mantle Light, P.O. Box 56, Cushing Rd., Thomaston 04681 (207) 354-6417

WELLS

Ocean View Cottages, P.O. Box 153M, Landing Road, Wells 04090   (207) 646-3308

Riverside Park, Wells 04090   (207) 646-3145

Stadig Mobile Park, RFD 2, Wells 04090   (207) 646-2298

Wells Beach Resort Campground, Box 655, Route 1, Wells 04090   (207) 646-7570

WESTBROOK

Highland Lake Park, RFD, Westbrook 04092   (207) 892-8911

Wassamki Springs Campground, 855P Saco Street, Westbrook 04092   (207) 839-4276

WHITING

Cobscook Bay State Park, Route 1, Whiting 04628 (207) 726-4412

YARMOUTH, NOVA SCOTIA

Doctor's Lake Campground, Dayton, Nova Scotia (902) 742-8442

Loomer's Campers Haven, Arcadia, Nova Scotia (902) 742-4848

Index